T0272298

We Few, We Academic Sisters

HOW WE PERSEVERED AND EXCELLED IN HIGHER EDUCATION

Edited by Betty Houchin Winfield
with chapters by Lois B. DeFleur, Sandra Ball-Rokeach,
and Marilyn Ihinger-Tallman

WSU
PRESS

Washington State University Press
Pullman, Washington

WSU PRESS

Washington State University Press
PO Box 645910
Pullman, Washington 99164-5910
Phone: 800-354-7360
Fax: 509-335-8568
Email: wsupress@wsu.edu
Website: wsupress.wsu.edu

Library of Congress Cataloging-in-Publication Data

Names: Winfield, Betty Houchin, 1939- editor.
Title: We few, we academic sisters : how we persevered and excelled in
    higher education / edited by Betty Houchin Winfield, with chapters by
    Lois B. DeFleur, Sandra Ball-Rokeach, and Marilyn Ihinger-Tallman.
Description: Pullman, Washington : Washington State University Press,
    [2023] | Includes index.
Identifiers: LCCN 2023037177 | ISBN 9780874224245 (paperback : acid-free
    paper)
Subjects: LCSH: Women educators--Washington (State)--Biography. | DeFleur,
    Lois B., 1936- | Ball-Rokeach, Sandra. | Ihinger-Tallman, Marilyn. |
    BISAC: BIOGRAPHY & AUTOBIOGRAPHY / Educators | EDUCATION / Professional
    Development
Classification: LCC LA2315.W3 W4 2023 | DDC 378.0092/2
    [B]--dc23/eng/20230905
LC record available at https://lccn.loc.gov/2023037177

The Washington State University Pullman campus is located on the homelands of the Niimíipuu (Nez Perce) Tribe and the Palus people. We acknowledge their presence here since time immemorial and recognize their continuing connection to the land, to the water, and to their ancestors. WSU Press is committed to publishing works that foster a deeper understanding of the Pacific Northwest and the contributions of its Native peoples.

Cover design by Brad Norr Design.

We Few,
We
Academic
Sisters

Contents

Dedication

To the many WSU faculty women who followed us as they too sought
new opportunities, chose new directions, and went
beyond our horizons.

Acknowledgments

This book would not have happened without the proverbial village for support and encouragement. A special thanks to Lois DeFleur's husband Jim McGorry and Betty Houchin Winfield's husband Barry Hyman for the Internet technical support as well as for constructive criticism and editorial guidance. We very much appreciate the Washington State University Press Editorial Board and manuscript readers who asked us pertinent questions and provided suggestions on how to enrich these stories. In particular, we applaud Washington State University Press editor-in-chief Linda Bathgate, who saw the worth of such a book a year ago and did all she could to move this project forward.

During the almost three years of the COVID-19 pandemic, we four retired academics met weekly via Zoom to share ideas and our writing and editing. Though illnesses, loneliness, and family crises, we, the authors, and this editor, valued those over one hundred Zoom discussions about our remembrances and our storytelling as well as our writing. Like sisters, we listened, sometimes argued, but supported each other with praise as well as criticism. We shared an appreciation of each other's sisterly support, but also proudly point to those women who followed us in breaking new ground for all academic women.

As they highlight in their chapters, the three sociology authors share a deep appreciation of the WSU innovators that broke new ground by hiring couples in the Department of Sociology. They remain especially grateful to the now deceased James Short and Wallis Beasley. They wish that these WSU leaders could have seen how all three, each in her own way, launched successful careers because WSU opened the door to them, over fifty years ago. During their WSU tenure, their husbands, Melvin DeFleur, Milton Rokeach, and Irving Tallman, substituted for the lack of female mentors while prodding these three female professors to be independent scholars and researchers.

Among their colleagues, they acknowledge others. Lois DeFleur is especially grateful to Provost Albert Yates who mentored her in administrative skills and provided the resources for Lois to advance her administrative career. Sandra Ball-Rokeach appreciated the opportunity to collaborate on scholarly publications with WSU colleagues James Short, Irving Tallman, Melvin DeFleur, Donald Dillman, and then doctoral student Joel Grube. Marilyn Ihinger-Tallman thanks Paul Reynolds who facilitated her transition from California to the Minnesota graduate program, and her colleague and lifelong friend, Gary Lee, who prodded her to apply for a WSU faculty sociology position. Marilyn also acknowledges John Pierce who as dean of the college mentored her when she became chair of the department of sociology. To paraphrase John Donne: no one is an island unto him/herself. As chair of the Department of Sociology Marilyn certainly did not do the job alone, nor could she have without the help of a wonderful group of women who always had her back. She wants to especially thank Margaret Davis and Peggy Flaherty for their unflagging competence and support as administrative assistants. Dorothy Casavant not only kept the department finances on track but was a great help to graduate students who needed a comforting shoulder and listening ear. These women were indispensable to the smooth running of the department. Isabelle Miller and Debbie Curan were the best student advisors any department could have. And lastly, the women who managed the front office, Sabreen Dodson and Donna Poire, put out many fires before they got as far as Marilyn's door.

Following their Washington State University time together, only Marilyn remained at WSU until her retirement. Betty Winfield left WSU for research fellowships at Columbia University and the Kennedy School of Government at Harvard before being hired by the University of Missouri School of Journalism. Lois and Sandra left for other campuses—Lois first to the University of Missouri and then to the State University of New York at Binghamton, and Sandra to the University of Southern California. They had too many colleagues, friends, and institutions who played important roles in their careers after the WSU years to thank here. Rather, they are acknowledged in the stories unfolded in this volume.

Finally, we recognize family members who supported us on our journeys from childhood to retirement. Lois's father served as a role model and her mother and sister, Carol, gave generous emotional support. Sandra's mother was a key source of encouragement as she broke away from traditional female paths. The Rokeach family took Sandra into their warm embrace. Marilyn's children demonstrated heroic accommodations to moves and changes and were her constant reservoir of a rewarding life. Editor Betty Winfield's friends, such as these three authors, and Joan Burbick, were her role models as well as mentors. She especially thanks her two daughters, Sidonie and Sharon, who were fans, as was her husband, Barry Hyman.

Foreword

Jeylan Mortimer
Professor Emerita, University of Minnesota

This is a truly remarkable book. Betty Winfield has performed a most valuable service in encouraging and supporting three academic "pioneers," Lois DeFleur, Sandra Ball-Rokeach, and Marilyn Ihinger-Tallman, in the telling of their life stories. The triumphs and challenges of these courageous academic women, as they attempted to enter and succeed in a nearly all-male academic world, are truly awe-inspiring. At a time (1960s and 70s) when women in the professoriate were rare (all three were the only, or one of just two or three females in their departments and other professional venues), these three managed to not only have successful careers, but to reach the heights of their fields as they became renowned researchers, academic leaders, and major award winners.

As one who entered the profession in the same era (early 1970s), I can attest to the veracity of their narratives. Given their prominence, I knew of each of these trail blazers, but only became friends with Marilyn Ihinger-Tallman when she was a graduate student, and I a new assistant professor, at the University of Minnesota. (Even then, her resilience and determination were awesome!) Anyone who doubts how far women have come in higher education need only peruse these pages to understand how difficult it was for mid-twentieth century academic women; their monumental efforts surely paved the way for their sisters in succeeding generations.

This book consists of three memoirs which provide revealing glimpses of what it was like to be a female academic at a time when women were generally not only unwelcome in the male preserve of higher education, but they also often faced outright hostility, harassment, and rules against "nepotism," which prohibited them from working in the same department as their spouses. Intertwined with accounts of their academic lives (dissertations, research projects, service on government panels, etc.) are highly personal revelations of their challenges, close personal relationships, anxieties, and losses. Since Betty Winfield provides excellent synopses in the introduction and concluding chapter, I will not provide such an overview here. Instead, I would like to convey some of my own reactions as I read the chapters.

First, it should be recognized that these three women's successes were highly unusual and broad-based. Their achievements extended well beyond sociology to academia as a whole; e.g., Lois DeFleur in higher education leadership, Sandra Ball-Rokeach as a renowned cross-disciplinary scholar, and Marilyn Ihinger-Tallman as Washington State University's first female sociology department chair. At a time when women were expected to confine themselves to their traditional roles as wives and mothers, they succeeded in the male-dominated sphere of higher education against all odds. How could they have done this? Clearly, their own personal qualities—their high levels of intellect, achievement motivation, perseverance, and resilience—contributed to their success. They also benefited from the hiring strategy of WSU's department of sociology leaders who recognized that opening up the department to professional couples would be helpful in attracting academic leaders to Pullman. Their own families may have also played a role, both their families of origin and procreation.

The accounts start off with descriptions of their early family lives. While their experiences growing up were markedly different, all three recounted how their parents, and sometimes siblings, prepared them for their future academic pursuits. Sandra Ball-Rokeach grew up in a stable family with a highly educated (PhD level), professional father. As her parents were immigrants to Canada from Great Britain, she became sensitive to experiences of prejudice and discrimination. Lois DeFleur relates how her father, who worked for the railroad, taught her the value of hard work. Marilyn Ihinger-Tallman grew up in a hard-pressed working-class family. Her mother loved to read, introduced her to books, and instilled a love of learning. However, her mother left the family when Marilyn was just 16 years old.

Family continued to be important to the development of their careers as the three entered academia. Each benefited from unions with more senior male sociologists who were crucial mentors early on (Milton Rokeach, Melvin DeFleur, and Irving Tallman). Because of the many strikes against them, their husbands' early guidance facilitated their early career trajectories, which led to opportunities for tremendous achievements thereafter. Interestingly, women who reached the pinnacle of the sociological profession in mid-century America, becoming ASA presidents, were also married to sociologists: Dorothy Swain Thomas, who became the first female president of the American Sociological Association in 1952 (W.I. Thomas), and, in the 1980s, Alice Rossi (Peter), Matilda White Riley (John), and Joan Huber (William Form).

Also noteworthy, none of the three Troika members experienced the most intensive phase of child-rearing (the infant period) as they climbed the academic ladder. Marilyn Ihinger-Tallman came closest, with an incredible balancing act of caring for five children in various stages of development as she proceeded through college and graduate education. But by the time she became an assistant professor at WSU her youngest child was entering her teen years. The other two did not bear children.

It struck me in reading these three riveting accounts that the vast majority of contemporary female sociologists do not have more senior sociologist husbands who collaborated with and mentored them during their early careers. Moreover, many young women sociologists perform highly complex balancing acts, caring for infants and preschool children while on probationary appointments, as they struggle to obtain tenure. It surely is not easy for them, but female sociologists today, while still suffering many of the problems experienced by these foremothers, enjoy heightened support from their departments and institutions. When Ball-Rokeach, DeFleur, and Ihinger-Tallman joined the profession, I believe university-sponsored day care centers did not exist, and there were few childcare centers of any kind. Contemporary women sociologists also have many more opportunities to bond with, and find mutual support from, women colleagues in their departments. As Winfield points out in the last chapter, today women constitute 49.6 percent of the sociology professoriate (while still having lower wages than men and less representation at the full professor rank). Of the most recent 25 ASA presidents,

14 are women. Women like DeFleur, Ball-Rokeach, and Ihinger-Tall-man surely paved the way, facilitating the success of contemporary female academics.

This book will surely be a source of inspiration for women, not only those striving to become sociologists or to succeed in academic careers, but those who are aiming for demanding professions of any kind. The three trailblazers offer helpful advice and guidance at the end of each of their accounts for contemporary young women who have high aspirations for success. Moreover, these three women's life stories show that attaining the highest levels of academic achievement, even in the most trying circumstances, is not incompatible with enriched personal lives, fulfilling friendship and love, and dedication to the wider community and the society at large.

Introduction

We Few:
Three Pioneer Women Sociologists

Betty Houchin Winfield

At the height of the 2020 coronavirus pandemic three longtime female professor colleagues and friends from our days at Washington State University and I moaned about being "locked-down" and suffering from "cabin fever." I suggested that since they, once so unusual as female professors who later became leaders and exemplars of academia, tell their incredible stories. As an incentive, I offered to run weekly Zoom meetings and edit their written accounts.

Thus, this book is the result of the past three years of Zooming, not just as tech novices, but also as survivors. No matter how terrible the epidemic around us or the physical challenges of one broken bone, toothaches, disturbing medical reports, family visits, and pandemic loneliness, we persevered. Through months and months of conversations and chapter drafts, we continued. All of us escaped COVID-19 as we wrote and shared stories.

Our connections are long and personal. They, these three sociologists, kiddingly calling themselves the "Troika," were longtime good friends and mentored me as an assistant professor in the then Department of Communication at Washington State University in 1979–1990. Even though they were sociologists, and I was not, professors Lois Defleur, Sandra Ball-Rokeach, and Marilyn Ihinger-Tallman took an interest in me and became my role models. They stood out, not just because they

1

were among the very few women professors at WSU, but also because the sociology department dared to hire three women.

In fact, by the early 1980s there were so few female full-time academics at Washington State University that we often met for potluck at one of our homes. I would sit next to an astrophysicist (the late Julie Lutz) and learn that some of the onerous university policies were campus-wide procedures, not just confined to my department or college. These three female academics along with an English professor friend Joan Burbick who had young children at home, offered survivor advice to me as someone who became the first tenured female in what is now the Edward R. Murrow College of Communication. In one sense, these supporters were allies who had my back and allowed me to be free as an individual.

A potluck dinner hosted by Lois (center) and attended by Marilyn (far left), Betty (right of Lois), and other women faculty, circa 1980. Sandra is taking the photograph.

Their support was personal as well as encouraging. During my eleven years at WSU, I met each of them in separate ways. My former Seattle newspaper editor, Liz Schensted, introduced me to her former WSU roommate, Betty Nyman, and husband, Jack, the then graduate dean, who often had me over for dinner with their friend, professor Lois DeFleur. Through the Nymans, I expanded my department contacts. After Lois became the first female dean of the College of Humanities and Social Sciences, she appointed me as co-chair of a campus-wide seventy-fifth birthday celebration for the renowned alumnus Edward R. Murrow. That three-day conference in 1983 brought in Murrow's wife Janet and noted scholars as well as major national broadcasters and journalists such as Diane Sawyer and former CBS news directors.

After the conference, Lois and I co-wrote *Edward R. Murrow: Challenge for the Future* (1986). Saturday after Saturday we spent writing and revising manuscript drafts, all while I kept weeping over a pending divorce. We also co-chaired a graduate student's thesis. And when my male department chairs hesitated awarding me an annual raise despite my strong review record, Dean DeFleur and her successor John Pierce overruled them. Over the years, Lois became a good friend and travel partner. In Mexico we explored Oaxaca and Puerto Vallarta, kayaked on the Sea of Cortez off Baja California, and enjoyed a week at Spa Rancho La Puerta. We also trekked in the Annapurna Mountain Range in Nepal to celebrate the new millennium.

Betty on the Annapurna trek in Nepal; photo taken by Lois.

The other Troika members were also career guides as well as good friends. Sandra Ball-Rokeach showed me that she valued my student mentoring during the WSU undergraduate research awards, which I continued to do for the rest of my career. She even put me on her graduate student's committee. Since her field of media sociology somewhat overlapped my specialty in historical media political communication, she offered encouragement, and we often touched base at national and international conferences.

Marilyn Ihinger-Tallman, a great listener, became a good friend and my after-work aerobics gym partner. Her husband, the renowned social psychologist Irving Tallman, would have dinner waiting for us afterwards. In 1990 when I received an offer at the University of Missouri, Irv offered to cook twice a week if I would just stay at WSU. 'Twas mighty tempting, I must say. During my last WSU semester, Marilyn used her frequent flyer miles to travel with me to Columbia, Missouri, to help me find housing.

By the mid-1980s two of the Troika took positions elsewhere. Lois moved to the University of Missouri as provost; and then, by the time I arrived at Missouri in 1990 she had become the president of the State University of New York at Binghamton. In 1986 Sandra left WSU for the University of Southern California Annenberg School for Communication as a distinguished research professor. In the thirty-plus years since then, we kept up with each other and enjoyed summer reunions in our home cities. The Troika attended Lois's and my subsequent weddings during the new century.

As this book will show, the Troika's education and early careers in the 1960s occurred while the country was becoming increasingly inclusive for women and minorities. Those years of social upheavals led to sociological studies of gangs, drug use, violence, racial unrest, student protests, family and gender changes, and mass media effects. Their stories during these societal changes deserve to be told from their experiences in graduate schools, their early academic positions, and as renowned scholars. Here, they provide not only historical accounts that parallel national trends and policies, but offer career case studies about women's talents, intellects, foci, and determinations from the 1960s through the first decades of the twenty-first century.

During the 1960s and 1970s the three women highlighted here—
DeFleur, Ball-Rokeach, and Ihinger-Tallman—dared not only to go to
college, but to attend graduate school, as they will tell. They were an
anomaly. It was a time when women were idealized as wives and mothers and homemakers, as scholars such as Stephanie Coontz recounted
in *The Way We Never Were: American Families and the Nostalgia Trap*
(1992). Sandra was engaged at the age of seventeen. Marilyn was married at the age of eighteen. On the cusp of greater gender career inclusion, they were pioneers. Marilyn had fully expected to follow a traditional role as a wife, mother, and homemaker until her marriage
disintegrated. Engaged or not, Sandra knew that she would become
an academic, never wanting a nine-to-five job. Lois's aunt and uncle
encouraged her to be an educator, but as a high school or junior high
teacher.

Certainly, to become a female professor was different. These women
foreshadowed the future changes, and they did so despite the graduate
school struggles of balancing a family of five children (Marilyn) and overt
sexism (Lois and Sandra). The 1960 US census found that only .06 percent
of American women had completed five years of college compared with 3.6
percent of men.[1] Women in graduate school were even more scarce until
the late 1970s, when American women began to earn more than half of all
bachelor's degrees and master's degrees and one-third of all doctorates.[2] By
2020, doctoral degrees have almost reached gender parity.[3]

The Troika's academic careers were highly unusual. As different as their
trajectories were, they each kept a focused drive as well as an ability to work
hard. They became full professors at a time when American women rarely
did so, even as late as 2015. At that time, 75 percent of all full professors were male. Scholars found that while women were hired, they moved
up the academic career ladder at a slower rate, were less productive, had
heavier teaching loads, and received lower salaries than men.[4] Not so with
these three women academics whose careers belie that finding.

In their early chapters they each tell of the nascent factors that contributed to their successes and the kinds of encouragements they experienced.
During the late twentieth century, they were in the right place at the right
time for vast societal changes and the inclusion of women. Universities
were becoming more diverse and recognized, even if begrudgingly, talent
and leadership, regardless of gender.

Early in their career paths the Troika tell of their arrivals at WSU as assistant professors, specializing in different areas of sociology: criminology and violence; media sociology; gender and family studies. By the mid-1980s, all three became tenured full professors. Cloistered in the WSU sociology department, they also became lifelong friends, sociology sisters. In their beginning chapters, they tell of their different childhoods, their educational efforts, their personal lives, hinderances, and career successes as they advanced. WSU was where their careers blossomed after initial starts elsewhere for two of them.

Their sisterhood meant that together they found outlets for their aggravations, anger, and stresses. As their stories indicate, traveling and attending concerts and festivals helped. Physically, they tested themselves and worked off their frustrations. Lois also found that strenuous physical activities and flying her airplane on the weekends were catharses. Sandra highlights taking care of her dogs and doing yard work as useful outside outlets. Marilyn points out that raising five children was a sharp realistic contrast physically, mentally, and emotionally to her academic career.

These three women garnered not just international reputations as recognized scholars, but also as academic leaders. Lois explains how she went through the professorial ranks and then the administrative ranks to become a dean, provost, and university president. Sandra points out how she gained an international status as a major media sociology scholar and leader. Marilyn discusses her progress toward becoming a well-known family sociologist and the first female sociology department chair at Washington State University.

These three women had many demographic similarities. In their stories they point out that they were Great Depression babies and came from American Caucasian families; two were from decidedly middle-class households, one from a family who struggled financially. Their families all valued education. All three, raised and initially educated during and right after World War II excelled as students in public schools and public universities.

Yet, these women also tell of significant family and class differences. Growing up in disparate parts of the country, their parents did not all have college degrees, or even high school certificates. Only one of their parents was college educated. Two of the fathers were professionals; one was decidedly blue collar. Two had families that moved extensively until after their college entrances. One's mother, frustrated and unhappy, left the family while her last child, this sociologist, was sixteen and still at home.

As pointed out, Marilyn married a year after high school and had five children before her divorce and first college degree. All three women married other professors, but two divorced and then remarried. Two became widows. These three completed their doctoral degrees and began their careers by sheer intellect, determination, and stamina. While they were married, they became individual scholars, known for their own research. They did this during the 1960s through the 1990s when they overcame numerous barriers including institutional quotas and nepotism rules, as well as overt sexual discrimination and sexual harassment. And yet, as they relate, they moved beyond these limits to excel.

The Troika's careers are examples of success during the American great social changes during the 1960s through the 1990s. One major marker was Betty Friedan's *The Feminine Mystique* (1963), which addressed the systematic sexism that relegated ideal middle-class women to the home, whether they wanted to be there or not. Only one of the Troika initially wanted to be relegated to a home and a family, as she will tell.

While the Troika grew up during the 1950s when the national aim was for a suburban middle-class culture, their mothers were very much part of the immediate post-World War II female homemaking life. Caucasian middle-class women had been discouraged from working or having careers once the men came home from World War II and were certainly different from the American women who had to work to support themselves and their families.

The country's postwar trend toward greater societal inclusion was happening as these women began and grew into their careers. Legal changes in the larger national culture set an agenda for inclusion and impacted their careers, directly or indirectly: the 1963 Equal Pay Act, the 1964 Civil Rights Act, along with Title IX (1972), which protected people from discrimination in employment and education based on sex. Their personal lives were also impacted. The Supreme Court validated women's right to use birth control (Griswold v. Connecticut, 1965) and with Roe v. Wade (1973) they were guaranteed reproductive freedom.

While the Troika had already begun their careers, by the time they were in their mid-careers, the United States celebrated the first woman in many areas. In 1980 only 8.1 percent of the country's lawyers were female when the first female federal judge was appointed in 1979; and then as an astonishing first that same judge, Sandra Day O'Connor, became the first female Supreme Court justice in 1981. By 1990 the percentage of all lawyers rose to 20 percent when Janet Reno, the first female attorney general, was appointed in 1993.[5] Other firsts were national, too, such as the appointment of the first female secretary of state in 1997, academic Madeline Albright, who had a doctoral degree. Such achievements established a national trend for female possibilities in all kinds of fields, including academia.

The national trends were also reflected in the sociology discipline. In 1969, the group that became Sociologists for Women in Society (SWS) met outside of the national American Sociology Association convention to discuss women's issues, and have an audience for gender-related papers, articles, and books on sociological study of either women or gender. As SWS members worked their way up the academic ladder, they also became part of the sociological powerful elite, broadened the content of journals, and expanded the college curriculum.[6]

During these national and professional changes, the Troika's amazing academic lives encompassed the slow but deliberate American inclusion and equality in other ways. Initially for two of the Troika, universities lacked the structural and socio-emotional support for female academics that universities later adopted. By the 1990s there was more national awareness of sexual harassment followed by—thirty plus years later—the subsequent avalanche of the #MeToo sexual harassment complaints in the new millennium. In their stories these three women address those issues. At the same time, they also noted that they did not operate alone; they had primarily male mentors who supported their dreams and encouraged their opportunities.

In this book, each Troika member tells her story in chronological order, starting with her childhood that pointed to possible clues of later academic successes, followed by her university education and career choices, and concluding with academic career and retirement. In each person's narrative, the Washington State University years are highlighted. These three female academics point to incidents at WSU that happened during the country's societal happenings: the lingering civil rights movement and racial riots, the university's attempts to achieve a more inclusive student body and faculty, and national student unrest over the Vietnam War. Closer to their careers were their personal lives in the isolated Palouse, such as the natural disaster of the Mount St. Helens eruption on May 18, 1980, and falling ash that covered much of eastern Washington, including Pullman and WSU.

Washington State University gave the Troika members numerous opportunities to gain experience and build careers. At WSU, they each began paths to renown, and WSU supported them as they moved forward. During their early academic careers, they mention that WSU had the flexibility to move beyond the usual campus nepotism rules and hired couples. These three women flourished as they balanced a career of teaching and research while at the same time dealing with personal family issues and medical crises.

The Troika's stories are salient reminiscences of lives lived in the latter twentieth century and first decades of the twenty-first century. For each narrative, their remembered past was never really past concerning the human experiences, as they recount. As recollections, their stories are by their very nature selective, each author's choices of what to include and what to omit. The Troika's continuity overlaps at Washington State University, 1975 to 1986, before two of them continued their careers elsewhere. Lois DeFleur's WSU years spanned 1967 to 1986; Sandra Ball-Rokeach's WSU time spanned 1972 to 1986; and Marilyn Ihinger-Tallman stayed decades, from 1975 to 1999.

Together, their accounts make a collective memory of academic life and female faculty careers in one academic area, initially in small university settings, and during the last half of the twentieth century into the first decade of the twenty-first century. By their very stories, the Troika define the challenges of being female professors and trailblazers. Despite trials and hinderances, and initially facing a lack of structural and societal support, these three women succeeded exceedingly well. Their reminiscences serve as important guideposts of meaning for the lives of women academics everywhere. Their experiences are markers of particular moments, at a certain time and in certain places.

The Troika stories resonate with the present, and as such become part of a collective memory of professors during fifty years of American academic life. French historian Pierre Nora explains the worth of such personal accounts: "the past never passes; those who took part linger on the scene, even as newcomers crowd their way in."[7] By uncovering the Troika's academic past, their stories can help newcomers as they make their way into the profession and create a social identity. They can learn what it is like to be a professor and have a full life, as did these three female trailblazers.

Notes

1. 1960 Census of Population, PC(S1)-37, table 173, https://www2.census.gov/programs-surveys/demo/tables/educational-attainment/1960/pc-s1-37/tab-173.pdf. Accessed June 8, 2023.

2. See Patsy Parker, "The Historical Role of Women in Higher Education," *Administrative Issues Journal: Connecting Education, Practice, and Research* 5, no. 1 (Spring 2015): 7, DOI: 10.5929/2015.5.1.1.

3. Educational Attainment in the United States: 2020, US Census Bureau, April 21, 2021, https://www.census.gov/data/tables/2020/demo/educational-attainment/cps-detailed-tables.html.

4. Parker, "The Historical Role of Women," 9.

5. Parker, "The Historical Role of Women," 9.

6. Heather Laube and Beth B. Hess, "The Founding of SWS," Sociologists for Women in Society, 2001, https://socwomen.org/about/history-of-sws/the-founding-of-sws/.

7. Pierre Nora, *Rethinking the French Past: Realms of Memory*, vol. 1: *Conflict and Divisions* (New York: Columbia University Press, 1992), 530–31.

Lois B. DeFleur

Chapter 1

My Childhood and Undergraduate Challenges and Growth

Several major threads run through my story. My midwestern family and early educational experiences provided an academic foundation for being a hardworking, ambitious professor and university administrator with the launching of my successful career at Washington State University.

I was born in Aurora, Illinois, in 1936. My mother was born in Yorkville, Illinois, and my father in Aurora. My mother grew up on a large, very productive farm, where they raised grain and had feeder cattle and hogs, which were fattened and then sent into the Chicago markets. My mother's family originally came to this country from northern Germany and settled in central Illinois, before my grandfather bought his farm outside of Yorkville, west of Chicago. My father was from a family that operated a small store, mainly aimed at the Scandinavian immigrants in the towns north of Aurora, since his family had emigrated from rural Norway.

My parents were raised in hardworking Lutheran families who wanted to get ahead and instilled these habits in their children. When my mother, the oldest child, graduated from high school, her parents sent her to a business school, where she gained office skills and quickly found an office job. However, when my father, the oldest, graduated from high school, his family needed support, so he went to work for the Burlington Railroad as a clerk. My parents met through some mutual friends and, after some time, married. They both worked hard at their jobs, and, after a few years, I was born, so then my mother stayed at home, and eight years later, my sister was born.

My sister's birth changed the family dynamics. I was accustomed to being the center of attention, so I would act out to get this attention. I picked fights with neighborhood kids and even, at times, would try to sic my dog Tuffy on them. Neighborhood parents complained, and then both of us would be grounded. It wasn't easy for me to adjust to having a much younger sister that everyone wanted to see and hold when, before, the focus was always on me. Since my sister is much younger, we never really became close when we were growing up. During her formative years, my sister didn't experience as much change as I did in terms of changing locations, schools, or friends.

My father was smart and a hard worker, so he was quickly promoted to jobs with more responsibility at various locations within the Burlington Railroad. We moved around a lot when I was growing up, living in Illinois, Wyoming, Texas, and Iowa.

Throughout my youth, my parents, and particularly my father, insisted that I learn the value of hard work, so, when I was six and wanted a bicycle, he said I had to earn half of the money. I took the lawn mower, which I could barely push, and went around the neighborhood trying to get jobs. Many times, the neighbors gave me a little money and said forget about the lawn. In high school, I worked in some fast-food joints and used the meagre pay for spending money. These jobs certainly convinced me that I needed additional education so I wouldn't end up in these jobs when I grew up.

My father was a very dedicated worker and spent whatever time was needed to do the best job possible. He often worked long hours and traveled frequently. When he wasn't working, he liked to spend time outside. In Wyoming, he frequently went fishing and hunting. When we took vacations, we would travel to areas where he could spend time out-of-doors. I always looked forward to these trips because I would be able to spend time with my father, and I also learned to love outdoor recreation.

As I said earlier, we moved frequently when I was growing up as my father was promoted to positions of greater responsibility within the Burlington Railroad. I admired my father, even though I didn't spend as much time with him as with my mother. However, I know that I was influenced by his attitude and values. He was supportive of me and often encouraged my independence. My mother was a strong and well-organized person. She would take care of all of the planning and execution of our relocations.

I recall that, during my junior high school years, girls were scheduled to take a home economics course, and boys were scheduled for a leather-working class. I definitely didn't want to take the cooking and sewing class (even then resisting the traditional female role). I complained to my father, who proceeded to talk with the teachers. They decided to make an

Lois's parents, Ralph and Isabel Begitske, 1978.

exception so that I could take the leather-working class. While the boys were making belts, the teacher had me design and make a purse for my mother. I was so proud of the purse, and, of course, my mother used it for at least a short period of time. Many years later, when we were cleaning out my parents' home, before my mother moved to a senior-citizen facility, I found this really ugly purse. I then realized that my mother had only used it to show her support for me, and we had a really good laugh about it.

I frequently was upset with these moves, because I would have to leave my newfound friends and have to adapt to a new school and new people. My mother would always say that the move provided new opportunities for me. However, the moves were difficult. There were always well-established groups in neighborhoods and schools who weren't willing to welcome a new girl into their group.

I grew taller than most of my classmates from junior high into high school. I kept growing, but I wasn't developing sexually. My mother took me to a doctor who prescribed hormone therapy, and this began to help me develop. However, it was most embarrassing when my first menstrual period began when I was in church. I was wearing a light-blue dress, and it was obvious to everyone what was happening.

I also remember my difficult adjustment when I first arrived in Burlington, Iowa, as a high school sophomore. Fellow students either ignored me or would make remarks about my height. I performed well in school, but I didn't have any social life. I had a part-time job at the telephone company to earn spending money. My situation changed when I made the girls' basketball team and we began winning games and went to the state tournament in Des Moines. As "the giant," six feet tall, I was able to guard the shorter players and often get baskets because I could shoot over them. Thus, I gained some positive attention and respect from fellow students.

During my high school years, my father was transferred again to take charge of the large Burlington Railroad facility in Aurora, Illinois, so we moved back there. I had decided that I wanted to go to college. My father said that I would have to work and pay for it myself, even though he had moved into a high-level management position with the railroad and earned a very good salary. Because he had worked so hard to advance his career, I believe he thought that this is what I should or could do.

However, I really wasn't sure. Also, I didn't receive any real help from the counselors in high school in terms of finding scholarships or financial aid.

Nonetheless, I was determined to go to college. I visited the University of Illinois, but it was just too big for me. It happened that my grandmother had a relative from the Yorkville area who taught at a small liberal arts college in southern Illinois. She suggested I talk with him. That is how I learned about Blackburn College in Carlinville, Illinois. I found out that it is one of eight "work colleges." This means you work on campus to earn money to pay for part of your college expenses. Compared to other work colleges, Blackburn is unique because the work program is primarily student managed. I decided to apply to Blackburn, and was accepted. However, they indicated that I wasn't eligible for student aid because of my father's income, even though he didn't intend to pay for my expenses. I paid for my tuition with my savings and summer work.

As a liberal arts college, Blackburn required students to take classes in the arts and sciences, as well as social sciences and a foreign language. I took Spanish as my language. I liked both my sociology and political science courses. At some point, I had to choose between them for my major, and I choose sociology, probably because the sociology professors were more helpful and supportive.

As freshmen, we all were assigned menial jobs on campus. I had to rise very early to clean several floors of our residence hall to get the job done before everyone wanted to use the communal bathrooms and other areas. After a year of this routine, I knew that I wanted a change. I learned that the work program was administered mainly by my fellow students, so I applied to be a work manager and was accepted. In the manager's role, you not only evaluated workers in the program, but also the work process. In my role, I evaluated the cleaning and small maintenance processes and implemented a number of adjustments.

At Blackburn, most students were in a number of student activity groups. Since I had played basketball in high school, I tried out for both the women's basketball and volleyball teams. However, the women's basketball coach was also the director of my residence hall. She convinced me to play basketball. I was the center, and I really enjoyed it. It was not all that demanding, since our opponents were primarily from other small liberal arts schools in the region.

To earn spending money, I also cleaned the homes of several of my professors. One of these was the home of my political science professor, whose wife directed the college theater productions. She asked me several times to try out for roles in these productions. I did, and I really enjoyed preparing and performing in these campus productions, such as *The Madwoman of Chaillot*, even though it required a significant time commitment.

During my junior year, I also cleaned the home of the college French professor and her economics professor husband. She talked to me about the need for a campus language laboratory, where students could listen to tapes and practice their language skills. Her husband also wanted his students in economics to do extra work that involved listening to tapes. They talked to the provost, and he agreed. I, along with a student from economics, ended up designing, equipping, and running a student listening laboratory. We found needed space in the basement of one of the residence halls. We worked with the maintenance department and their student workers to design the laboratory, order the equipment, and have the equipment installed. By then, we were put in charge of the laboratory operations.

My work experiences as an undergraduate helped me develop organizational and leadership skills. These skills helped to prepare me for administrative roles that I would assume later in my career. Best of all, I enjoyed the challenges. Looking back, I realize that it was in my family

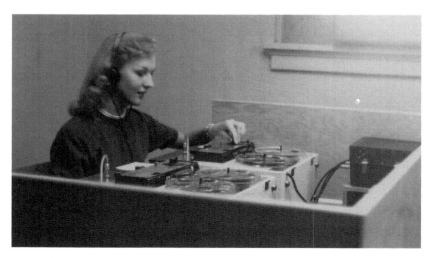

Lois in the language lab she set up at Blackburn.

where my basic attitudes and values were developed in terms of honesty, respect for others, and the importance of hard work. Also, my father was pleased with my choice of Blackburn College for my education. He was proud when I became a member of the "management team," i.e., the Work Committee. Encouragement from my family and mentors on the faculty at Blackburn led to my later successful years in graduate schools, as described in my next chapter.

The Blackburn Work Committee with Lois on the front row, far right.

Chapter 2

Graduate School and Hard Work

The faculty at Blackburn took great pride in advising and mentoring students. In my senior year, my sociology and political science professors talked with me about my future plans. I wasn't sure what I wanted to do with my sociology major after graduation. Since I had been an assistant residence hall director at Blackburn, my sociology professor suggested that I apply for the Student Personnel Administration Graduate Program at Indiana University. After graduation from Blackburn in 1958, my application was accepted at Indiana University.

The university also gave me an assistantship to serve as head resident of one of the smaller undergraduate residence halls. Its location happened to be next to the residence hall of the university football team, and the players were dating the young women in my residence hall. During some bed checks, I would find some of the players in bed with the women. They could be very threatening when I told them to leave. This was, of course, in the era of many housing regulations regarding visitors and hours. As the head

Lois's Blackburn graduation photo, 1958.

resident position also included the role of enforcer of all those rules, I had major challenges! Despite my height and determination, there were constant problems and issues in this role. I quickly became disillusioned about my future in student administration.

Also, as a graduate student in the School of Education, with no prior classes in education, I needed to take some basic classes at Indiana that I did not find very interesting. I discussed this with my advisor, who also happened to be the wife of the chairman of the sociology department in the College of Arts and Sciences. She arranged for me to meet with him about the master's degree in sociology.

The meeting with the chairman seemed to be going well, until he commented that the department hadn't had much success with women persevering through the program to completion of the PhD degree. They quit or married. Somehow, I was able to convince him that I was different and would see it through. After this meeting, I was able to transfer to the graduate program in sociology.

My first year in the sociology program, I received a teaching assistant-ship and, thus, was able to end my time as a residence hall director. I was assigned to help Professor Albert Cohen with his juvenile delinquency classes. One thing I noticed right away was the significant number of very tall young men in the class. I quickly learned that they were members of the Indiana University basketball team. They had some tutors assigned to them who met with me to ensure that the students were on track and focused on the main concepts in the course.

Then, about halfway through the course, Professor Cohen left to accept a special grant. I was then told that I would be the primary instructor for the rest of the semester. I developed the remaining assignments and tests. The first test that I wrote was probably tougher than it had to be. Many of the basketball players failed it. The next day, I received a visit from two assistant coaches from the athletic department. They made it clear to me that I would bear the responsibility of the university's basketball program's decline if the players weren't able to pass the course. I sought some advice from Professor Melvin DeFleur, and he recommended that I prepare tests that were easier to pass. I did so.

In my second year at Indiana University, Dr. DeFleur offered me a research assistant position on a project investigating how young people learn about occupations and the role of TV in this process. I enjoyed interviewing forty-seven young students to gather the needed information. I then worked with Professor DeFleur to analyze the data. I was also able to use some of the data for my master's degree thesis. The findings of the project were that the beginnings of the children's concepts regarding specific occupations started before the child enters first grade. The children continue to learn that specific and complex skills are involved in many occupations. The young students also had the idea that jobs are arranged in some type of hierarchy of prestige.

During this time when I was collaborating closely with Professor DeFleur, we became romantically involved. He was married, and this situation was very difficult for both of us. After receiving my master of arts degree at Indiana University, I transferred to the University of Illinois for my PhD work.

Before I left Indiana University, I had met one of Professor DeFleur's doctoral students, Pedro David from Argentina. As a member of the Fulbright Commission of Argentina, he encouraged Dr. DeFleur to apply for a Fulbright Award at the University of Cordoba, located in northwestern Argentina. Mel DeFleur received the Fulbright Award, and he divorced his wife. He and I married and headed to Argentina before I began my course work for my PhD at the University of Illinois.

As a sociologist, Pedro David also had contacts at the Instituto de Sociologia at the University of Cordoba, so I was able to work with the institute on a large research project focused on juvenile delinquency issues in Cordoba. This complex project involved gathering information and data from the police, the provincial jail, juvenile courts, and the provincial census office. The institute supported and facilitated the project and its field work.

Meanwhile, my Spanish language ability improved considerably and quickly. I was gathering data about the motivation, socio-economic backgrounds, gang organization, objectives, influences, and judicial consequences of juvenile delinquent male gangs in Northwestern Argentina. A then-current theory of my former Indiana professor, Dr. Albert Cohen, was that such gang behavior was a result of a delinquent subculture. Yet, in my research, I found that this was not applicable to gangs in Cordoba. Rather, the delinquency was organized theft by poor young males, distanced from dysfunctional families, jobs, schools, and churches, acting for personal gain. The Instituto de Sociologia allowed me to take my data back to the United States to analyze.

Lois with Melvin DeFleur, in front of their new Kentucky home in the
mid-1960s.

Upon my return to the United States in September of 1962, I began my PhD work at the University of Illinois. I worked hard to complete the required course work, pass the required doctoral examinations, and show proficiency in the required two foreign languages. Since much of the sociology literature was in either French or German, these were the languages in which I was expected to be proficient. However, I successfully petitioned to have Spanish, rather than French, as one of my languages because I planned to use the data and interviews gathered in Argentina for my dissertation.

During this time, Mel DeFleur left Indiana University and was hired as a professor for the University of Kentucky in Lexington. I was still working on my dissertation for the University of Illinois but was hoping to get work in or near Lexington. Colleges and universities at that time generally had nepotism rules, and so the University of Kentucky would not hire a married couple for their faculty. Luckily, I was able to obtain a teaching position in Lexington at Transylvania University, a four-year liberal arts institution. Even though I had a heavy teaching load of four courses a semester while there, I completed my dissertation and earned my PhD from Illinois.

While in Lexington, I also decided to pursue a long-held dream of learning to fly. As a young girl, I read with great interest about the early women pilots who achieved great satisfaction from developing and exercising their aviation skills. I went out to the Lexington Airport and enrolled in the flight training program as the only woman. The instructor who agreed to provide my training continually evaluated my dedication and abilities. Would you believe: On my first flight with him, he put the plane in a spin! Then he said, "Do you still want to do this?" This just reinforced my determination to earn my pilot's license!

One of the requirements to get the Federal Aviation Administration (FAA) private pilot license is to have several solo cross-country flights. Usually, these are accomplished by flying several "out-and-back flights"—flying from your "home" field to another airport, landing, and then flying back. I had scored 98 percent on my FAA pilot's written examination, which was the highest score in my class. With that, and knowing that I was employed full time, my instructor recommended that I complete the cross-country requirements in one day. I did all the necessary flight planning, and then, on the target day, I flew from the Lexington airport to the

Cincinnati airport. After refueling, I took off again and flew to the West Lafayette, Indiana, airport and again refueled. Next, I flew to the Louisville, Kentucky, airport. After landing and refueling, I took off on the last leg, back to Lexington. After this exhausting day of flying, I was treated with much more respect by my instructor and classmates.

Several months later, I had my FAA private pilot's license. I started renting planes to explore Kentucky and the surrounding states. Mel flew with me regularly. I talked him into taking flight lessons, and he also obtained his pilot's license while we were still in Kentucky.

Chapter 3

Early to Mid-Career:
Professor to Administrator

In the beginning of my academic career, I started focusing more on scholarly papers and publications. For example, in 1966, while still at Transylvania College, my paper "Assessing Occupational Knowledge in Young Children" was published in *Sociological Inquiry*. I knew that I needed scholarly credentials to be hired by a doctoral research university. At that time, there were very few female role models or mentors for guidance. However, throughout graduate school and my early career, Mel DeFleur had been both my husband and mentor and was very supportive of my developing career. And I remembered that, during my undergraduate education at Blackburn College, there were several women professors who supported and encouraged me, so I was confident that I could succeed in my future endeavors.

I was fortunate to have one of my papers on juvenile delinquency in Argentina accepted for presentation at the annual American Sociological Association meeting, the most prestigious conference in sociology. My paper, "The Development of Delinquency Theories Applicable to Other Countries," was accepted in a juvenile-delinquency session chaired by Professor James F. Short of Washington State University. Impressed by my work, Dr. Short was also familiar with Melvin DeFleur's publications in mass communications, and he initiated discussions with us about possible positions at WSU in Pullman, Washington.

WSU, like most universities at that time, had the anti-nepotism rule that prevented a related couple from being in the same department.

When we went to Pullman for interviews, we met with the sociology department and with Provost Wallis Beasley, also a sociologist. Impressed with us, he said that he would work hard to hire us both—which he did.

In 1967, we headed West, with Mel's appointment in sociology, and a joint appointment for me in sociology and rural sociology as an associate professor. This meant that I had an appointment across two different colleges with two different administrations: the College of Agriculture and the College of Humanities and Social Sciences. This challenging arrangement was exacerbated by my now large research project on patterns of drug use and law enforcement in Chicago that I had developed after my Argentina work. This project stood in sharp contrast to the agricultural focus of the Department of Rural Sociology. Soon, the administration recognized this research disparity in rural sociology in the College of Agriculture and justified, in 1969, moving my appointment full-time to the Department of Sociology in the College of Humanities and Social Sciences. There, I had colleagues in my fields as mentors, such as Jim Short, a nationally known sociologist.

Certainly, some faculty members worried that having a married couple in the same department might result in them becoming a "voting bloc" and dominating department discussions and decision-making. In time, our sociology colleagues came to realize that Mel and I developed positions independently, and their fears were assuaged. I think our success in integrating into the department helped set the stage for recruiting other married professors to WSU.

With Pullman in a rather remote area of Washington, Mel and I bought a Piper Cherokee aircraft so I could keep flying. We enjoyed exploring the Washington countryside on weekends.

In those early years at WSU, I continued to work hard on teaching, with new courses and more sociology-focused students. The later 1960s and early 1970s included the anti-Vietnam War protests. WSU ("Wazzu") students often wanted to talk about the war and demanded to make statements in the classroom. I would give them ten minutes before we moved to that day's scheduled topic.

Mel became chairman of the sociology department in 1971, and in 1972, he recruited professors Milton Rokeach and Sandra Ball-Rokeach. They were both prominent social psychologists, and Sandra had worked with Dr. James Short on the Violence Commission.

Lois and her first airplane, 1968.

During this period, I kept working on my research and gave numerous papers in national conferences. I had published a number of scholarly articles before WSU Press published my book, *Delinquency in Argentina* (1970). Meanwhile, as I was establishing a strong professional identity as a sociologist, I began working with graduate students. By the 1970s, I became the director of a federally funded, doctoral-training program at Washington State University. This program was intended to improve recruitment and retention of graduate students. It also entailed the development of special courses and applied research experiences. With this emphasis and special seminars, more than twenty-five students completed their PhD degrees under this program. As example of the program's applied focus, I worked with one student on a project about occupational knowledge among high school males. We flew in my plane to many Washington cities and towns to interview over 300 male students (from some twenty-two high schools) regarding their adult occupational choices and preferences.

In 1973, a university-wide committee selected me to give the campus-wide 33rd Faculty Invited Lecture. My lecture, "Perspectives on Urban Drug Problems," was presented in the huge Bryan Auditorium to a large audience. I talked about my Chicago research.

By 1975, I was promoted to professor of sociology, the first woman to achieve this rank in my department.

Also in that year, the department hired Professor Marilyn Ihinger from the University of Minnesota. Marilyn's husband, Professor Irving Tallman, was hired as a

Lois at WSU, 1975.

visiting professor in the fall of 1976, and he was hired permanently a year later.

As I advanced professionally, problems developed in my marriage to Melvin DeFleur. I was no longer his student working on his directed projects. I had become increasingly independent and was being recognized for my own scholarly accomplishments. And another, younger, tall, blonde graduate student had caught his eye, as my dad had once predicted. Our seventeen-year marriage ended in divorce in 1976.

It was a devastating time; Betty and Jack Nyman, friends of Mel and me, remained supportive of me as our marriage was falling apart. I spent holidays with them and their extended family. I also often joined them for dinner at their home. After Betty Winfield joined the WSU communications faculty, she connected with Betty Nyman through a mutual friend, and, subsequently, I met Betty Winfield at the Nymans' home for those dinners.

My friendships also included Sandra Ball-Rokeach and Milton Rokeach and Marilyn Ihinger-Tallman and Irv Tallman. After my divorce, they too remained friends with me.

After workday hours, I started making a routine of working out at the gym daily with Marilyn Tallman and Betty Winfield. Afterwards, I would often enjoy the hospitality of Marilyn and her husband Irv for dinner.

I often would also enjoy Sandra and Milton's hospitality. The dinners were great, but, even more important, these friendships were particularly strong social supports for me. These close friendships with Sandra, Marilyn, and Betty continue to this day.

Uncomfortably, Mel and I remained as colleagues in the Department of Sociology, attending faculty and committee meetings for several months. Then, in 1978, he left for a position at the University of New Mexico (with my blonde former doctoral student).

For about seven more years, Mel and I continued working on new editions of our sociology textbook with co-author William D'Antonio. *Sociology: Human Society* was published by Scott Foresman in 1972, and it was the best-selling college sociology textbook. It was followed by subsequent editions in 1976, 1981, and 1984. This textbook, adopted by many colleges and universities for undergraduates, required many author communications and meetings before each revision. In our writing, we developed the text sections and chapters between the three of us before giving them to the publisher's editors. To facilitate the coordination, we met in a wide range of locales during school breaks to focus on the work without the usual academic interruptions.

Following our divorce, and with pending subsequent editions, Mel grew increasingly uncomfortable working with me and wanted me out. Fortunately, Bill D'Antonio and the publisher insisted that I remain.

As I continued flying, I decided to use my textbook royalties to purchase a new, faster, and more complex (e.g., retractable landing gear) aircraft—a Piper Comanche 260C. Then, as the single owner, I was able to fly often around Washington state, sometimes with the Rokeaches or the Tallmans or Betty Winfield as my passengers. We had a lot of fun together. I also took longer trips to Chicago to visit family members. In addition, I flew to Alaska and Mexico a number of times for academic meetings and vacations.

On one of my three trips to Alaska, I was attending a PAC-12 meeting for the Arts and Sciences deans at a lodge in the Denali National Park, which had a nearby grass strip where I landed. While there, a dean from a certain university (in the town of Berkeley, CA) was a bit too attentive. During a break in a meeting, I wanted to check on my plane. He insisted on walking with me through the woods to the airstrip, "for my protection." As the path curved to the right, suddenly, there was a full-grown moose on the path, facing us about fifteen feet ahead. It had really bad breath, and it didn't look happy. I started talking to it in a low, slow voice, while slowly backing up. Then I heard a loud rustling sound behind me. I looked back, and I saw my would-be "protector" running away as fast as he could. Big help! I continued to back away from the moose, getting a little more space. At some point, another noise got the moose's attention. That's when I turned and ran back toward the lodge. When I got there, I saw my colleague (that jerk) in the bar, telling the guys about "his" encounter with the moose! I said, "Thanks a lot! You were a big help when you ran from the moose."

Our textbook, *Sociology: Human Society*, changed the trajectory of my career. It became quite successful and was adopted by many colleges and universities. It was used in courses at the US Air Force Academy. Included in the textbook was my brief bio, which mentioned that I was a pilot and owned an airplane. The Air Force Academy noticed. In 1975, when the service academies were planning the integration of women, the superintendent at the Air Force Academy contacted me regarding the possibility of being the first female distinguished visiting professor (1976–77). This

Lois teaching at the US Air Force Academy, 1976.

prestigious position appealed to me both as a sociologist and as a pilot. I accepted the appointment.

During my time at the academy, as a professor teaching classes, I had a quite different pedagogical experience, especially the first day of classes. When I entered the classroom, all the cadets jumped to attention before the cadet section leader shouted, "All present and accounted for, Ma'am!" I was then to respond, "At ease! Take your seats." Surprised, I had not been prepared for that class procedure. I smiled! What a contrast to the usual university classroom!

While in Colorado Springs, I was able to conduct some research about the integration process, as well as fly. In my off hours and on weekends, I happily flew several jet trainers, such as the Cessna T-37 "Tweet" and the supersonic Northrup T-38 "Talon."

I collaborated with several young captain instructors to gain data regarding gender integration to try to understand the successes as well as the challenges during this historic time. This research revealed that, in contrast to the other service academies, the Air Force Academy did not punish as strongly for sexual harassment as did West Point, among other differences. My report became the basis for change. I realized that I had made a major difference in gender integration there.

After my year at the academy, I returned to Washington State University. Now, as one of the few female full professors, I continued to participate, as well as lead, many university-wide activities and committees. At the same time, I became more prominent nationally because of my research and publications. I was also more active in national education associations. I served on their boards and was elected to leadership positions. For example, I was elected president of the Pacific Sociological Association (1980–82). Later, when I was the WSU dean, I served as the president of the Council of Colleges of Arts and Sciences (1985–96).

While still in Pullman, I continued flying my airplane on the weekends. One particularly memorable flight was on May 18, 1980. Early that morning, I flew to Spokane with a friend. We landed at Felts Field, a general aviation airport where I kept a small car. We drove across town to Fairchild Air Force Base, where there was a major air show. It was fun seeing the latest military aircraft, including the SR-71 Blackbird—a Mach 3+ high-altitude reconnaissance aircraft.

After a brief time, we noticed that the late-morning western sky was turning dark. I immediately called the FAA Flight Service Station to assess the weather. They told me that at 8:30 a.m., Mount St. Helens, in southwest Washington, had erupted. Furthermore, those massive dark clouds were ash moving northeast across the state. We hurried back to Felts Field to put my plane in a hangar and then began driving back to Pullman in the blinding pelts of very dark fine ash. It was nearly zero visibility, and we had a tough time just staying on Highway 195. It took more than five hours to go the eighty-one miles to Pullman. And we both ingested a lot of volcanic ash.

The Pullman area accumulated several inches of ash, which significantly affected the university. Students were told to stay in their residence halls. Most faculty members tried to get to their offices. Within hours on the first day, the administration cancelled all classes for the rest of the semester. Fine ash was getting into the then exceptionally rare and expensive electron micro-scopes. The next week, the campus was to go into the formal examination period. The administration left the exam schedules up to individual depart-ments and faculty members. They allowed students to take their course grade to-date or to go ahead and take the final exam as scheduled. For my classes and with student agreement, I gave students their course grades to date. This national disaster was devastating, not just for Pullman in Whitman County, but for the state: The ash left considerable damage across the State of Wash-ington and beyond. All the roads into and out of Pullman were closed, except for the highway south into Lewiston. The eruption killed 58 people and destroyed 250 homes, 47 bridges, and 185 miles of highways.

For the fall of 1980, Washington State University awarded me a year-long sabbatical leave to be a visiting professor of sociology at the Univer-sity of Chicago. Besides teaching a graduate seminar on deviant behavior each semester, I was to finish the writing and editing of several research projects, including my study of the integration of women at the USAFA. This leave became a productive time for me academically, concentrat-ing on my research and on the technical report on my Air Force Acad-emy year. During the spring of that year, momentous events occurred at Washington State which again changed the direction of my career.

Before traveling back to Chicago that Spring 1981 semester, WSU was trying to fill an administrative vacancy—dean of the College of Humanities and Social Sciences. I had been nominated for the position and completed interviews, but WSU selected a University of Wisconsin professor who had prior university administrative experience. However, his wife and family were not enthusiastic about living in the Palouse area of Washington after years in Madison. He spent a year at WSU as dean, but he informed the upper administration that he was returning to Wisconsin at the end of the 1981–82 academic year.

The university now faced a dilemma of how to fill this administrative position. My campus colleagues informed me that the president and the academic vice president did not really want to conduct another search. They had discussions with the search committee about offering the dean's position to me. A few days later, Dr. Glenn Terrell, WSU's president, called and asked me to meet him at Chicago's O'Hare Airport for a discussion about the dean's position. He argued that the position would be a good fit for me, but I would need to return to Pullman a couple of months earlier than I had planned. After much discussion, I finally agreed to return in June to assume the dean's position.

While I had some administrative experience, as chair of university committees and the PhD federal training grant, it clearly was not comparable to assuming responsibility for Washington State University's largest instructional college. The Humanities and Social Sciences College consisted of twenty departments and programs with over 300 faculty and thousands of students. Due to my familiarity with the campus and after working with faculty administrators on campus committees, I felt somewhat comfortable assuming the dean's position.

Thus, I began my tenure as dean in 1981, and I felt that I needed more in-depth knowledge of individual departments and programs in the college. I had designated visits where I gathered information about each unit's goals and issues. Through these visits, I gained a lot of knowledge about the college's organizational culture. As dean, I reported to the new university provost, Dr. Albert Yates, who had been recently hired to replace long-time provost Wallis Beasley, who had retired.

I was the newest member of the Dean's Council, along with the deans of the other colleges, including the deans of the professional schools, such as the Colleges of Business, Veterinary Medicine, and Agriculture. Once again, I was an outlier. The only other women serving on the Dean's Council were in traditional female fields, such as the dean of the College of Nursing and the dean of Home Economics.

My first year as dean was quite challenging. I was learning more about the many fields represented in the college, as well as the many administrative procedures. In my meetings with the provost, Dr. Yates was incredibly supportive, but he could also see that I lacked significant administrative experience. He told me about a summer program at Harvard University that he had attended, which was particularly good training for new administrators. So, after discussions with him and President Terrell, the university agreed to sponsor me to participate in Harvard's Institute for Educational Management in the summer of 1982. This joint program of the Harvard Business School and the Graduate School of Education was demanding, with lots of reading and homework, but extremely useful. It broadened my perspectives and helped me learn how to better support the departments and programs in my college. I also learned about the value of national data for context and decisions. Throughout my time as dean, Provost Yates acted as an informal mentor to me, and he was always willing to talk with me more generally about academic administrative issues.

One of my early tasks at WSU was to learn more about the colleges, especially the faculty demographics in each department, in contrast to national statistics for potential faculty. The College of Humanities and Social Sciences had a poor track record for inclusion. After gathering national data regarding the availability of women and minorities in the various fields in this college, I strongly urged some departments to increase their hiring of women and minorities. There was some pushback on these efforts, but Provost Yates supported me.

For example, when the English department had a vacancy and began their recruiting efforts and selections, they came to me with three chosen male finalists. I urged them to look carefully at the national data showing a considerable number of potential women candidates fitting their specific criteria. They adamantly pushed back and argued that these were their chosen candidates. Period. When I refused to budge, they said that they would go to Provost Yates, implying that I would be overruled. Yates, as an accomplished chemist and an African American, responded by calling for a meeting that included me.

There, the English department committee talked at length about the difficulty of finding qualified women and minorities for this English subfield. The provost listened, then pulled out the data (my research copy) that showed the availability of women and some minorities in that vacant area. He very strongly urged them to work harder on their recruitment efforts. They did so grudgingly, and eventually hired a woman.

Regrettably, during that first year of my deanship, the State of Washington was hit with an economic downturn that created great budgetary stress for the university. All the departments and their programs had to grapple with financial reductions. We also considered some organizational realignments, which many faculty opposed…and not quietly. Unfortunately, we had to close the theatre program. It was also necessary to combine departments. Among these were speech communication, which was joined with the mass communication department, and the social work department, which was combined with the sociology department. Lots of unhappy faculty complained and let me know their grievances.

Probably most satisfying for me as dean was learning more about faculty accomplishments, as well as the future academic plans of departments and programs. For example, I learned from Professor Betty Winfield of the new Department of Communications that the late Edward R. Murrow, a nationally known reporter and radio broadcaster, had graduated from the university. In 1983, Murrow would have had his seventy-fifth birthday. She thought it would be fitting to organize a symposium exploring how Murrow and his standards and accomplishments provided a foundation for the future development of the country's mass media. I appointed a university-wide planning committee. In April, we held a three-day conference entitled "The Edward R. Murrow Heritage." Sessions covered the changing industry; news values, past and present; Murrow, the man; the dilemmas of war coverage during Murrow's World War II era, and during the Beirut battles; the ethics and morality of news coverage now; and the challenges for the future. This conference garnered a lot of regional coverage. All sessions were packed with students, faculty, and visitors.

The Edward R. Murrow Heritage Conference was extraordinarily successful as the most extensive Murrow symposium to date. It included all the then-current and former CBS News presidents, as well as prominent national broadcasters and scholars. The then CBS Morning News anchor, Diane Sawyer, gave the keynote address on the future of broadcast news. Afterwards, Professor Winfield and I wrote, edited, and published *The*

Edward R. Murrow Heritage (1986). This book analyzed and summarized aspects of Murrow's journalism values and legacy, as highlighted in the conference panels and speeches.

During those five years as dean of an exceptionally large and diverse college, I learned a lot about many academic areas and faculty specialties, as well as the college staff and the students. To be a good leader, I had to be open and strong. While there were always many challenges as well as successes, WSU broadened my academic horizons considerably as a leader. I participated in regional and national meetings of administrators, chairing panel discussions, and making presentations where there were very few women and minorities represented.

After a few years as dean, I began to get inquiries regarding other positions—particularly for openings as academic vice president and provost posts at other public universities. I explored several of these. In 1986, I accepted the provost position at the University of Missouri, in Columbia, Missouri.

The attraction of the provost position at the Missouri-Columbia campus was in part because the campus chancellor, Dr. Barbara Uheling, was a strong woman and very impressive. Also, it was the largest and most complex campus in the University of Missouri System, with the system office in Columbia, not far from the campus.

Once again, I moved and purchased a home and took my airplane. Not long after arriving, I met with all the deans of the university's schools and colleges, which included the Schools of Medicine, Law, Engineering, and Journalism. I also visited most of them to gain additional information on their strengths and weaknesses, as well as their goals.

However, I soon learned that Chancellor Uheling was in trouble in terms of support on campus and in the system. Unfortunately, four months after I was hired, she resigned. The president of the University of Missouri System appointed the Columbia campus financial vice president as the interim chancellor. This was difficult for me because he did not have an academic background and did not understand the parameters of that part of a university.

In the meantime, I continued to focus on immediate academic issues. For example, the university had received a federal directive of deficiencies in the recruitment, retention, and support of African American students. The state demographics showed almost 12 percent African Americans in 1980. To help address these issues, I recruited a talented African

American academic as associate provost: Professor K. C. Morrison. He developed initiatives to help departments and colleges address the federal directive. He also visited with many prominent African Americans in the state's cities to gain their ideas and support. As a result of these efforts, we were able to meet the federal directives, and we also recruited additional talented African American students to the campus and worked on hiring minority faculty.

During this time, there were significant reductions in state support for the university. The Provost's Office collaborated with the schools and colleges as they developed plans to make their operations more efficient, while continuing to offer quality educational programs to students. This was a challenging period for the university. Some majors and programs with small enrollments were reorganized or eliminated. The College of Public and Community Service was shut down, but with continuity of academic programs through other university colleges. All the deans worked hard on the efforts to streamline their programs in the face of resistance to changes and reductions. Some directors and deans resigned or left the university. During my tenure as provost, I recruited new deans for the Schools of Law, Medicine, Arts and Sciences, and Business and Public Administration, as well as Nursing and Engineering. For example, in the School of Journalism, a new dean was recruited to help strengthen and coordinate their professional offerings with their academic coursework.

Within a period of months, Dr. Peter McGrath, the president of the University of Missouri system, recruited a new Columbia campus chancellor from Texas A&M University, Dr. Haskell Monroe. Haskell worked hard to help me solve academic issues and develop some new programs.

I often flew my plane during holiday breaks to the Aurora, Illinois, airport, which was quite close to where my mother and sister still lived in Yorkville, Illinois. My father had passed away from pancreatic cancer in 1980, while I was still at Washington State University. Still feeling that loss, I wanted to spend more time with my family, and it was an easy trip, flying my plane from the Columbia airport to Aurora. My sister Carol was looking after our mother and taking good care of her. It was during this time that I began to feel a lot closer to my sister, and we established a great and lasting friendship.

During my time as the provost at Missouri, I continued some scholarly work, as well as my involvement in several professional organizations, such as serving on the Executive Committee of the Academic Affairs Council of NASULGC (the National Association of State Universities and Land-Grant Colleges) and the Commission on Minorities of the American Council on Education.

After a few years, I began to receive inquiries about presidential positions. I explored several of them and sometimes found that I was an affirmative-action candidate and was not treated as seriously as the male candidates. This was discouraging. However, in 1990, I was contacted about a presidential position in the State University of New York (SUNY) system at one of their doctoral research universities: the State University of New York at Binghamton. And, there I went. The next chapter will cover the many challenges and accomplishments of my years at Binghamton.

Chapter 4

Late Career:
Up the Administrative
Ladder to President

In my research of the State University of New York at Binghamton, I learned that this former Harpur College was the newest of the doctoral/research campuses in the state. With seven colleges, it was still developing in terms of its size, range of degrees offered, and level of research. At first I didn't know a lot about the campus or the exceptionally large State University of New York system. I interviewed initially with the local governing board—the University Council—in Binghamton, New York in early 1990. They, as well as the State University trustees (in Albany), were appointed by Governor Mario Cuomo. I enjoyed talking with this group, which included several extraordinarily strong women. I thought the interview had gone well, and I was pleased when they called me and said they were recommending me for the presidency to the SUNY System Board of Trustees.

So, a few weeks later, I traveled to Albany, New York, for the interview with the Board of Trustees. It went well, but several trustees quizzed me about being a Midwesterner and whether I could make it in New York. I was confident that I could, and I told them so. And, surprisingly enough, they were particularly impressed with my pilot ratings (private pilot/commercial pilot/instrument rated). I was offered the president's position at Binghamton University. In July of 1990, I flew my plane from Columbia, Missouri, to the Binghamton, New

York, airport, where I had arranged for a hangar. I walked across the airport and took a commercial flight back to Missouri to continue my move.

One of the reasons I was attracted to Binghamton was because of its roots in Harpur College—a high-quality liberal arts institution. Also, its location in the Southern Tier of New York State was the early home for IBM and other high-technology firms. For many years, the state senator for this area had been one of the most powerful in the state. He worked hard to have one of the four SUNY doctoral research institutions located in the Southern Tier. Thus, Binghamton, as a young university, had a solid foundation for growth.

I was in awe of the beauty of the area. The Binghamton University campus is incredibly attractive, with green fields and rolling hills. The 930 total acres includes 600 undeveloped acres, and the core of the undeveloped land constitutes the Nature Preserve: 190 acres, including a twenty-acre wetlands area (with a beaver pond), plus several miles of multiple hiking and running trails. Certain classes meet there, and it is called "the largest and best-used laboratory on campus." The preserve is home to deer, beaver, fox, muskrats, porcupines, and other mammals, plus various amphibians, and reptiles, and over 200 bird species. Also, it is open from dawn to dusk for students, faculty, and visitors, except for a few days each year when the access path is closed. Thus protected, the yellow-spotted salamanders cross the path going to and from their spawning grounds.

I sold my house in Columbia and, after discussion with the Binghamton Council, we decided that the current president's home, which was off campus and hadn't been occupied by the outgoing president, needed significant renovations. It was preferable to give me a housing allowance for a private residence. I found an almost-new house in the woods, about five miles from campus, that had privacy, and the first floor was relatively open in a design that would work for official entertaining.

One of my first tasks at Binghamton was to recruit a good team of vice presidents to help me develop and prioritize my objectives as president of the university. The outgoing president was immensely helpful in providing initial information regarding his vice-presidential team. He also had recruited a faculty member as a member of his office staff. This long-time member of the history department was thoughtful and knew the university faculty very well, so I asked him to stay and provide me with information about the campus.

The university provost had been a candidate for the president position, so I did not think it was a good idea for him to remain in his position. He reluctantly agreed, and he returned to his faculty role. In the meantime, I also met with all the deans: an impressive group.

I began meeting with many local business leaders, and I joined the largest Rotary Club in the area. For the most part, everyone was very welcoming and were pleased that I wanted to be a part of the local community. At that time, New York, as well as many other states, was experiencing major fiscal challenges. However, while there were financial issues, Binghamton was able to move forward on hiring and other initiatives. I immediately began to strengthen the university's small Foundation and add staff so that we could increase private fundraising. I quickly learned in meetings with some alumni that, since Binghamton was a state institution, they felt they should not have to contribute to the university. I could tell that I would have to develop a culture of giving back to the university.

Our students were both vocal and active in clubs and causes. For example, not long after I arrived in fall 1990, the physical facilities department recommended that we temporarily close one of the undergraduate residence halls (and move the residents to other residence halls) so that needed repairs could be made more quickly. However, the affected students had different and very strong views about moving. They then carried several of their beds into the lobby of the Administration Building and occupied the lobby continuously for a few days. They said that they would not leave until they were allowed to return to their residence hall. As the days passed, campus police were apprehensive about having the students in the building over the weekend. I decided that Saturday morning to meet with the student demonstrators. I told my plan to the campus police, and they were nervous about it, but I went ahead. Unannounced, and clad in sweatshirt and jeans, I arrived. The students were quite surprised when I walked into the lobby that morning, sat down, and asked them to talk with me about their issues. After about an hour of their very vocal complaints, they decided that they had made their point to the person in charge, and, satisfied, they left. Whew!

In any state-run school system or university, I knew from past experience that it was particularly important to establish and maintain good relationships with key agencies and political figures in the state capital, and that may be especially true in New York and the surrounding states. I worked with Governors Mario Cuomo, George Pataki, Eliot Spitzer, and David Paterson, and their staffs. I also collaborated with the speaker of the state assembly, Sheldon Silver, plus local members of the state assembly, as well as with the US senators from New York: Hillary Clinton and Charles Schumer.

Even in challenging fiscal times, the state legislature continued to make construction money available, so many union workers continued working on college projects. People seemed happy, and the campus benefitted from the construction of new residential communities, academic buildings, and the university's new downtown center.

Lois receiving an award from New York Governor Mario Cuomo, 1994.

Legislators also wanted to hear directly from students and faculty, not just the president, so we developed a special "Binghamton Day" in Albany. We would take a small group of faculty and students by bus to the capital for scheduled meetings with legislators and their staffs. And we would host a reception for them, before we returned to our campus, almost two hours away.

I was at an advantage that I had my own plane and could fly to and from Albany for various meetings while reducing my "time on the road." My flights also supported meetings at other SUNY campuses, plus America East athletic conference meetings.

While I was a university president, I was elected chair of the National Association of State Universities and Land-Grant Colleges (1995), as well as the American Council on Education (1998). I genuinely enjoyed these leadership roles and learned a lot from other administrators.

A colleague and friend, Joan Wadlow, was president of the University of Alaska at Fairbanks. In May 1999, she invited me to present the commencement address at her university. I turned this event into a brief family trip to explore Denali National Park, including a flight around Mount Denali, landing at its base.

Early in my tenure as president of Binghamton, I had the vice president for External Affairs work up a plan to strengthen our ties with alumni so that we could develop that culture of "giving back." He and I travelled widely to meet with groups to energize Binghamton alumni and ask specifically for their support, including financial support. We convinced them that extensive state funding was a thing of the past. Many alumni and supporters wanted to help undergraduate students attend Binghamton, so we were able to raise money for scholarships. We held events where we honored the scholarship students, as well as their donors.

Binghamton had always had a reputation for strong undergraduate programs, and it was consistently listed as among the national rankings of the best undergraduate colleges. However, as one of the four doctoral research universities in SUNY, it needed to enhance professional and graduate programs, both with students and faculty. We worked hard to do this.

At the same time, we continued to enhance and build new undergraduate residential communities with Faculty Masters who were the hallmark of student living at Binghamton. The Masters helped the students enhance programs for their communities. There was also healthy athletic competition between the residential communities. Alumni would always ask each other, "What was your community?"

As far as collegiate athletics, the University of Binghamton was an NCAA Division 3 school for intercollegiate athletics when I arrived. I

A family trip to Denali, Alaska. Lois (right) with (from the left) her sister Carol, brother-in-law Don Bennett, and mother Isabel Begitske, 1999.

took our school to Division 2 and then Division 1 in a two-year period. We did not field a football team, but we established basketball (and other sports) in the America East Conference, along with the SUNY universities at Albany and Stony Brook, and other northeastern universities. Unfortunately, soon after that transition, we had some basketball players get in trouble for shoplifting, which led to their dismissal and the firing of their overly protective coach. The program "rebounded" well after that very public embarrassment.

As the numbers of undergraduate students increased toward 18,000, we also established new residential communities with the more modern suite living. These areas had their own dining facilities, as well as areas for student activities.

Binghamton students are carefully accepted (32 percent acceptance rate). Before I retired, there were over 148 undergraduate programs with an 82 percent graduation rate.

The provost and the dean of the Graduate School planned new graduate degrees, but this was more challenging, as many graduate students needed support to attend their programs. The provost worked with the deans of the schools and colleges to develop more support, despite the slow process. Several graduate programs already had ties with international universities, and we enhanced these programs. We visited several colleges in Turkey to try to increase the numbers and fields for their students to attend Binghamton and have success. Our Anderson Center for the Performing Arts brought in additional international performing groups to our campus, which was very much appreciated by the campus and the community. In fact, we hosted several international festivals, focusing on Scotland, Ireland, and Turkey. These included performance groups and lectures that enhanced our academic programs.

The horrendous terrorist attack on our nation on September 11, 2001, had a strong impact on our campus. Many of our students were from New York City, as you might expect, and a significant number had friends or family numbers who were first responders (firemen or policemen) or were employed in the World Trade Center towers. One of our Binghamton alumni had his insurance company on one of the upper floors, and he employed quite a few other grads.

The attack took place while I was in a senior staff meeting, so we immediately started to plan campus responses. The provost announced that professors could cancel their classes or adjust them to discussions about the attack. We reached out to the Student Association, and they wanted to hold a remembrance and vigil that evening on the campus center quadrangle, with representatives of the administration, faculty, and staff. Later that day, the Binghamton mayor and other local officials reached out to my office to find out whether we were planning a joint remembrance event. We set that up for that Friday, including those officials, me, and representative members of the local clergy. It had a large attendance, and it was very moving.

In 2005, we established a downtown campus in the city of Binghamton for our College of Community and Public Affairs (CCPA). We had acquired a suitable property in 2003, and we constructed a state-of-the-art building for our faculty and students. The CCPA is still going strong and building a national reputation.

In June 2006, the Southern Tier region of New York experienced a major natural disaster when the Susquehanna and the Chenango Rivers, which merge in downtown Binghamton, flooded and displaced hundreds of residents. The local Red Cross asked the university to try to accommodate the evacuated people. We set up hundreds of cots in our Event Center, and we

Binghamton University president Lois DeFleur and US Senator Hillary Clinton talking with flood victims, 2006.

had our food service prepare basic meals for these hundreds of people. Our US senators, Hillary Clinton and Charles Schumer, visited our facility and told folks that there would be federal aid. This occurred between the spring semester and the start of the summer session, so the university was able to focus on the flood victims. Community and political leaders were very appreciative of our efforts to help the flood victims.

Due to its proximity to New York City, the university also benefitted from visits by many celebrities for various events. Harry Belafonte, the New York Philharmonic, Sidney Pollack, Willie Nelson, Melissa Etheridge, NYC mayors, and New York State governors and US senators performed in the Anderson Center or spoke at graduation ceremonies, etc. The glass walls at the back of the Anderson Center's large auditorium can be opened to accommodate even larger crowds on the grass hillside beyond.

All during my presidency, the campus continued expanding its graduate and research programs. Departments and colleges were receiving more funds to support their faculty research and needed more space for these activities. The university had also just been awarded funding for a Center of Excellence in Small-Scale Systems in Engineering.

This was also the time when the New York State Electric and Gas Company, located on a large parcel of land across the street from the campus, needed to consolidate their administrative space. They were moving into a newer, single building on their property that could accommodate more computers and fewer people.

The university began discussions with the company for the purchase of most of the land and the large building which was being vacated. The company would continue to own the smaller parcel of land with the smaller building and parking space around it. To assist in our expansion efforts, some parts of the larger building were suitable for our administrative activities, and some parts could be used for non-laboratory research.

As soon as the agreement was completed, the university began planning the construction of two buildings on the property. One was for engineering classrooms and laboratories, and the other was for the Small-Scale Systems Research Center of Excellence. We were quite happy with the results.

In 2009, there was an airshow at the Binghamton airport, and the US Navy Blue Angels aerial demonstration team was the major attraction. The airport manager called me and said that the Blue Angels were offering a VIP ride in a two-seat F-18 Hornet. In my nineteenth year as the university president, I qualified. Would I like to have that VIP ride? You had better believe it! I grabbed the opportunity, and I have the pictures to prove it.

Lois preparing for takeoff in a Blue Angels F-18 Hornet, 2009.

By 2010, the university, which started out as Harpur College in a single building in Endicott, New York, had become a major doctoral research university with strong undergraduate and graduate student bodies and faculty (including a Nobel Prize–winning physicist). It has a well-earned international reputation. When I retired in 2010, after twenty years as president, I felt proud of what I had accomplished at Binghamton University. It had taken a full commitment of time and energy over these years.

In the years following my divorce, I had developed close relationships with several different men whom I cared about. Yet, as I assumed more demanding university administrative positions, it was quite difficult to spend the time needed to sustain those relationships. Thus, I had been single for more than three decades when, in 2009, I met the father-in-law of the faculty professor whom I had just assigned as my deputy in the President's Office. We had some common interests. Jim McGorry had graduated from the US Air Force Academy. He was also a combat fighter pilot who had flown the F-4 Phantom II during the height of the Vietnam conflict, and he was interested in aviation in general. It didn't hurt that he was also a physicist, an expert skydiver, and stood six feet, five inches. In fact, after talking with him, I invited him to go flying with me the following weekend! We kept in touch after he returned to Denver, Colorado, and we began a long-distance relationship. A year later, when I retired in 2010, we married. We kept flying, usually once or twice a week, weather permitting. Life is good.

Lois and her husband Jim McGorry, 2022.

Epilogue

Glancing Back, Eyeing the Present, Looking Toward the Future

Looking back to my undergraduate days, I was interested in both sociology and political science, but ended up majoring in sociology. However, I still didn't have a clear vision of careers in these two fields when I was considering what direction I might take after graduation. After Blackburn, I headed to a program in student personnel administration at Indiana University. However, as I stated earlier, my experiences in this program weren't as gratifying as I had anticipated, so I went back to sociology as a graduate student and professor's assistant at Indiana, where I earned my master's degree. I still had no clear career goal, yet I continued in graduate school, assuming it would benefit me in whatever career I pursued.

Then, during my research assistantship with Professor Melvin DeFleur, who would become both my supervisor and mentor, he encouraged me to continue my education toward a PhD in sociology. As I progressed, I knew that an academic career would be intellectually challenging and working with both undergraduate and graduate students would be rewarding.

Other issues awaited, once I completed my PhD in sociology at the University of Illinois. By then, I was married to Melvin DeFleur. We were an "academic couple." At that time, most universities had anti-nepotism rules, so we couldn't be employed in the same department or, often, in the same college.

It was through the creative efforts of the Washington State University administration and, particularly, Professor Jim Short, that we were both hired there in 1975. In addition to my husband, Professor Short became my informal mentor. Soon, I was appointed to college and university-wide committees, and Professor Short helped me become active in the Pacific Sociological Association, as well as the American Sociological Association. The relationships with colleagues from around the country helped me develop a broader reputation. Still, there were relatively few women colleagues.

My third mentor was Provost Albert Yates, with whom I worked while I was dean of the College of Humanities and Social Sciences at Washington State. (He later became the president of Colorado State University.) He helped me develop good administrative skills when I was appointed dean, and he supported me attending the Harvard Institute for Educational Management.

I cite the above examples to illustrate the importance of mentors in my career development. It was a welcome change when the Tallmans and Rokeachs and Betty Winfield were hired because Marilyn and Sandra and Betty became long-term friends and, to some degree, mentors. Even now, I believe it is more difficult for women to find good mentors, particularly in some male-dominated fields.

My appointment as dean of a large college at Washington State marked a significant change in my career and was unplanned in terms of my aspirations. I would advise women not to reject out of hand significant opportunities, even though you might have concerns regarding your specific preparation for a position. Women need to have confidence in their broader abilities, and they may still need to work harder to get ahead. As my father used to say, "Women need to work twice as hard to be thought of as half as good as men."

Women also need to be aware of the informal relationships and networks that develop in groups, since these have impacts both on the individuals and on the functioning of the group, through decisions on resource allocations, and other actions.

When I was dean, I heard about poker parties that several of the deans hosted, which included the provost. I asked one of the deans about this, and, seeming somewhat embarrassed, he said that these were just small, informal get-togethers. I asked if I could be included, and he said yes, if

I was a poker player. Of course, I wasn't, but I accepted this as an invitation. Then my challenge was to learn quickly the basics of playing poker. Two of my friends helped teach me, and I went to the next party. All the males seemed somewhat on edge (a bit "off their game"), as they smoked cigars and drank bourbon (they knew I preferred scotch). It was a long night, but, after that, they treated me with more respect. I was invited to subsequent poker parties, but, somehow, I always had a schedule conflict. It became a standing joke among us.

I took a risk attending the poker party because I strongly believe that women also should be risk takers and willing to take advantage of both expected and unexpected opportunities. My career benefitted significantly from such opportunities. Fortunately, today there are more opportunities for women in higher-education fields, and they are able to take advantage of them without learning poker.

Looking back, I recognize that my diligence and my competitive drive to succeed, coupled with my willingness to take risks and accept challenges, were essential to my career. Eyeing the present, I would recommend my career path to younger women. Looking forward, I would do it all again.

Sandra
Ball-Rokeach

Chapter 5

The Childhood Years:
Primitive Origins of a Sociological Mind

My story has five threads for the next five chapters: (1) why I became a sociologist; (2) seeking an academic career in sociology in the 1960s and early 70s before the women's movement took hold in academe; (3) Washington State University as a launching pad for my career; (4) aspects of personal life that affected my journey; and (5) selected theory and research work I undertook during my fifty-three-year career.

Setting the stage for my personal and professional development was my birth in 1941 to parents who had emigrated from their homelands in England to take up residency in Ottawa, Canada, in 1937. My mother, Ailsa Mary Neill Ball, came from a working-class family in Manchester. She had little more than an elementary school education, while dad, Leslie Wilson Ball, had a PhD in physics from Manchester University. Their improbable meeting occurred because mother's sister, Evelyn, was a nurse working at the Manchester University Hospital where she met her future husband, Philip. Philip and dad were both physics students at the university. Philip proposed a double date, he with Evelyn and dad with mom. Ailsa was quite a looker, as they used to say, and she was a charming extrovert. Leslie had a boyish charm and was quite handsome. Mom and dad went hiking together all over the English countryside. As I recall, a storm brewed that prevented them from getting back home one day, forcing them to sleep over in a barn. It didn't take long for the romantic relationship to develop.

Dad was an only child in the resort spa city of Buxton in a nouveau riche family. Their rejection of my mother probably motivated my parents to immigrate to Canada the day after their marriage in 1937. Dad had received an offer from the National Research Council based in Ottawa to join a team of physicists who were developing one of the first uses of cobalt radiation therapy for cancer patients. Ottawa is the capital of Canada, but it was quite provincial at that time. Mother at the age of twenty-one began to implement her goal of having four children before the age of thirty. My older sister was born in 1939, and I was born in 1941.

In Ottawa and for the remainder of their lives, their friends were highly educated professionals. For example, Ottawa neighbors and close friends included the parents of Margaret Atwood. Margaret was born in 1939 to noted entomologist Carl Atwood and his nutritionist wife, Margaret, or Meg as my mother called her. Mom was the best correspondent I have ever known and that meant that the Atwoods and many others remained lifelong friends. I guess Margaret Atwood and I were together as infants, but I was only a few months old, so have no memory of that. When Margaret and I were in our forties, I did meet her briefly when mother and I visited her mother, Meg.

My mother was often asked where she went to college. She never got over the insecurity that goes with not being able to answer that question in a way that made her equal with their friends. I admire her adaptation. She learned that people liked nothing more than talking about themselves. Mother would preempt conversations by asking questions about the other person, thereby avoiding as much as possible having to reveal that she never went to college, much less high school.

Sandra's parents, Ailsa and Leslie Ball, in the 1930s.

Knowledge of the consequences of my parents' class differences sensitized me to this and other structures of inequality. Additional features of my childhood prompted me to be an outsider/insider observer of the worlds I encountered—a perspective that I suspect was central to my becoming a sociologist. As odd as it may seem, our family experienced prejudice when we immigrated to the United States in 1942. A vivid early childhood memory was the strange experience of being called "Ball'ed headed Chinese" by antagonistic children on our block. The veritable Victorian British ways and accents of my parents obviously made us stand out as different. Being the second born of four children, I took on the typical role of intra-family negotiator. I pleaded with my parents to let us be more American. For example, I fought with my father to let my younger brother wear jeans instead of the short pants that English boys used to wear well into their adolescent years. Those short pants brought visibility to our difference and trouble for my brother, being ridiculed and bullied by his contemporaries.

We were a nuclear family with no extended family in the United States. We had an upper middle-class income from my father's salary. Our wealth came solely from owning a home. Being on our own, we had to develop a deep streak of independence and self-sufficiency. Of the values my parents instilled, those I most treasure are independence, a certain irreverence, honesty, tenacity, and the importance of a sense of humor in hard times. These values and experiences served me well in adapting to frequent family moves, having to adapt to new places and schools. We landed in Burbank, California (1942–44), and subsequently moved to Silver Spring, Maryland (1944–51), Altadena, California (1951-57), and finally to El Cajon, California (1957–59) where I finished my last two years of high school.

A major reason for our frequent moves was that my father was too much of an independent and outspoken cuss to be a company man. His career went from being a physicist adapting cobalt for cancer treatment to working on the development of the atom bomb and ended up largely in the space industry as a high-level executive addressing systems reliability. After the bombing of Hiroshima and Nagasaki, my father went around the country arguing for the peaceful uses of atomic energy. He was an articulate speaker able to communicate science to a lay audience.

At the age of fourteen, my mother had to leave school to help with family finances and worked as a telegrapher. For most of her married life, Ailsa worked in the home handling four children and becoming embedded in whichever city she found herself. Moves were very hard on her. As the family moves cumulated, mother went from idolizing my father to becoming aware of his limitations. Probably most important was her increasing knowledge that while she could make and keep a circle of close friends, dad could not do so in the workplace. He did not learn how to express his disagreements with company policies in a politically savvy manner. He had a quick mind and expressed what he saw as a stupid idea in an unfiltered manner. Nonetheless, his brilliance in the arenas of his work meant that he would get quality offers from other agencies or companies, so that he never went without a very good job.

Our family life was not particularly a happy one. My parents being influenced by their Victorian upbringing adopted the position that children should be seen and not heard. This left us kids to fight for attention and with each other. The only family member that would keep us bound together was our dog, Kim. I would talk to him about my problems and never go anywhere without him. He always protected us. On one occasion in the woods behind our home in Silver Spring, Maryland, he confronted a poisonous snake (a copperhead) to warn me. Fortunately neither he nor I were bitten. This is not to say that my parents didn't try to provide support for us. For example, dad built a sledding trail in the woods behind our home in Maryland, and he built a badminton court in our yard in Altadena. Mom insisted that we join a private club in Altadena so that we could play tennis and swim. She was deathly afraid of the water, but would stand watch over us as we swam in the ocean off of the California coast. Nonetheless, there was a lot of conflict and lack of mutual support among us four kids.

For my part, our frequent moves meant that I had to learn how to go from being the new kid to having a group of supportive friends. Friends and teachers thus became central to building my confidence and self-esteem. I often think fondly of the teachers who took an interest in me and prodded me to excel and to become a student leader. One memorable seventh grade teacher in Altadena, California, Mr. Sogomonian, gave me a leadership role in his core class that he ran like a court. I was the prosecutor enforcing good behavior. He also encouraged me to run for vice president of our class. I did, and I won. I went on to hold one or another student government office through to the high school years—John Muir in Pasadena and later at El Cajon Valley High. In this sense, I was more like my mother than my father.

As time went on, I would say that I took on some characteristics of each of my parents. My mother taught me how to overcome my inherent introversion to make friends. I wanted to model her spunk and curious mind. Dad taught me to be analytical. Over the dinner table, we would be asked to explain how refrigerators and many other things worked. I think it is fair to say that I took on his outspokenness and willingness to challenge prevailing ways of thinking.

NEW ASB OFFICERS—Commissioners for next year's ASB are, left to right, Betty Webb, cultural affairs; Mei-Ling Bauer, publicity; Patty Chavez, public relations; Sandy Ball, vice-pres.; Chris Nordenson, finance; Elora Ayers, secretary; Elaine Molsberry, school service; and Bill Christiansen, athletics.

Sandra Ball as El Cajon Valley High School student body vice president with her fellow officers, 1958.

I am glad that my parents had neither the inclination nor the resources to place me in a private school. I think I learned more about structural inequalities by being in a public school. Despite being accepted in my White world, my insider/outsider observer positioning sensitized me to class and racial/ethnic prejudice in my K-12 experiences. In my Altadena junior high, I saw a vice principal run off a Black youth from entering the school grounds. I can still see that event and feel the confusion it triggered in me, not to speak of the anger it provoked in the youth. At a primitive level, I knew it was wrong. On another occasion, I was the instigator of disrupting a class by having all of us bunny hop out into the hall and back into the classroom until I ran into the face of the vice principal. There were many phone calls to parents figuring out how to punish us. In the end, the administration decided that I would just have to go home for a day, but my lower class compatriots would be suspended for a week or so. Knowing that this was wrong, I refused this classist prejudice and wouldn't go home until either I was suspended or all of us got away with going home for a day. The administration relented and we all went home for a day. I got the most hurtful comeuppance when I learned that our beloved dog, Kim, died that day at the age of eighteen.

In my first two years of high school (1956–57), there was only one public high school for all of the wealthier and poorer parts of Altadena and Pasadena serving a diverse array of races/ethnicities and social classes. I saw teachers in this high school congratulate a White student for answering a question while ignoring basically the same answer previously given by a Latino or Black student. I befriended a few students of color and lower class students and was invited to their homes in far less affluent areas than the one I lived in. To my dismay, my parents would not allow me to bring friends of color to our home. Sensitivity to class and racial prejudice were thus instilled early as I negotiated my own identity.

There was a fair amount of both agonistic and acted out violence at my Pasadena high school, including fist fights, tearing off females' pierced earrings, and the occasional knifing. On one occasion, a group of Black females circled me after a football game at the Rose Bowl. They were readying to beat me up until several Black students I knew approached and told the others to back off, saying that I was okay. So, this tall blonde and blue-eyed White girl learned how to bluff meanness when threatened with physical aggression, but also to trust that the "other" can be a friend.

My experiences at El Cajon Valley High School (1957–59) were quite a different story. I went from a diverse environment in Pasadena to a largely White and middle- to lower-class community. The primary ambiance was one of a ranching and military community where most of my classmates did not intend to go to college. I found the change appealing for its less competitive and mostly good-tempered nature. Most of the friends I made were the daughters and sons of ranchers, military personnel, or local government officials, such as the son of the fire department chief.

I was having a good time in my core class when the vice principal suddenly came in and pulled me out of that class saying I didn't belong there. He had just received my scores on the various tests I had taken and proceeded to put me into an honors class in my junior year. I told him that I liked the class I was in, but he was insistent. There were smart and fun students in the honors class, but I believe I am the only one that would go on to doctoral studies. I was dating and popular enough as indicated by being elected vice president of my class in my senior year.

All in all, it was a good experience, but one incident stands out that both informed and saddened me. A wonderful and popular friend of mine became pregnant. Once this became known, she was summarily ostracized and called a whore by other students, particularly by males. The gender inequality that allowed high school males to brag about their sexual conquests, but stigmatized females if they became known as easy lays became a stark reality. In 1959, the world did not acknowledge this or many other kinds of sexism. There was no feminist social movement at that time. This experience sent the message that males could be promiscuous, but females had better be virginal or suffer the consequences.

During the summer in between my time at the two high schools, I learned another lesson about being a female. From adolescence to that time, I had been what you would call stocky. Due to my being athletic, I was strong and solid, but not the slim body type. My mother even took me to a place where they used passive machine exercise as a way to slim girls and women down. That did not work for me. I decided in the summer of 1957 to put myself on a diet that consisted of eating what I wanted from breakfast to noon and fasting for the rest of the day and night. I can remember the hunger pangs. They receded after awhile and I was rewarded with considerable weight loss.

My body image changed from stocky to one of a five-feet, nine-inches slim girl. I went from having almost no waist to having a sleek silhouette. My mother was pleased. The lesson I learned came from the reaction of boys as I entered my new El Cajon high school. It is not as if I had not dated earlier, but all of a sudden, I was sexy and sought after by my male classmates and college guys who were part of my friendship network. While I enjoyed the attention and certainly had sexual attraction to these males, I experienced a felt difficulty. My inner thought was that I was the same person inside, but the outside changes in my body image made one heck of a difference and that upset me. I did not like the idea that males, though pimply and stocky, were still acceptable sex objects, but not females. So, remembering what happened to my pregnant friend, I kept my libido under control.

Probably my least virtuous attitudinal and behavioral pattern in childhood was the outright disrespect I showed to those whom I did not see as having authority over me. This included the poor babysitter or the public school teacher. If I decided that a babysitter was lame, I wouldn't obey the order to go to bed or otherwise behave. I still feel guilty for humiliating a teacher in elementary school by encouraging the whole class to disregard him. For example, I orchestrated a scene where we all looked up at the ceiling at 2 p.m., totally ignoring the poor man. It is true that he was a terrible teacher, but it took me the years of overcoming the meanness of children to reflect upon his humanity and to acknowledge my role in harming him. As I look back, the sociologist in me interprets this as the difference between authority and power á la the classic nineteenth-century sociologist, Max Weber. Weber taught me that authority is legitimate power and that when legitimacy is lost, all you have is raw power that can be contested. And contest I did, with little empathy for the subject of my disregard.

Teachers that I respected in the world of religion played multidimensional roles. My parents, Leslie and Ailsa, were raised Anglican and could never quite find a Protestant substitute, going from Methodist to Presbyterian to whatever. In adolescence I became quite involved in a Pasadena-based Presbyterian Church where I participated in and even lead a Bible study youth group. Several adults in that church took an interest in me and gave me good counsel as I struggled with the common problems of adolescence. Probably the most unique problem I was having was a value conflict I experienced as a member of a clique who had started to party, smoke, and explore sex. My parental and religious training stood firmly against what was considered the behavior of the wild crowd. In talking with my adult church counselors, I discussed my felt difficulty in continuing to hang out with this clique. With their supportive advice, I broke those ties. I can still remember the anxiety I felt the first time I had school lunch completely on my own, mystifying the clique by not sitting at what had been our table. As time went on several other members came to join me at the lunch table, breaking their ties with the clique and becoming some of my closest friends.

Questioning religion nonetheless emerged and grew to serious proportions when I was fourteen years old. Those questions focused around the teaching I had done in Bible study where I found it harder and harder to accept the literal understanding of Jesus. I asked for a meeting with the minister to pursue a rather basic question: Could I be a Christian if I did not believe in Christ as presented in the Bible? His kind, but definite, answer was no. This began an unraveling process that led to my dropping out of the church that had been so kind to me. I became a fourteen-year-old agnostic and soon became an atheist.

Around this time, my father had given up on going to church services, saying that he was a pantheist and found God in nature. This laid some of the groundwork for my subsequent spiritualism. I began to ask the more fundamental question of whether or not I believed in a God. When I was sixteen, I happened upon Loren Eiseley's 1957 book, *The Immense Journey*. It speaks to the flow of life as it takes place in geological time. From that point onward, my spiritualism was more geological than theological. I see parallels between geology and sociology with their shared ecological approaches to multiple layers of forces of construction and destruction or change and conflict.

An ecological perspective also grew out of the fact that from an early age I was outside of the house as much as I could be, exploring and enjoying nature. I loved the mountains and their mysterious forests with ever-changing light. In one place we lived, our house was set just in front of the woods where all kinds of fauna could be encountered. Much to the dismay of my parents, I deployed the baby carriage they had given me to carry around dolls to, instead, bring back snapping turtles and frogs ensconced in sand or mud. Thus, my deviation from traditional gender roles was evident at an early age. It was also evident in the sports I played. I was one of two girls on the boy's hardball team and loved it until the boys caught up with the growth and strength of young girls. So, then, it was tennis, swimming and softball.

As I approached the end of high school, I came to feel the support of my mother for continuing to deviate from traditional gender roles. My father thought of me as a sweet girl who would make a good wife and mother. He once told me that I would make a good secretary, so I purposely got a C in typing class. Given their differences in educational attainment, this seems incongruous. I should note, however, that my mom had a high level of native intelligence. From her I learned that people with little education could be very smart. Mother would seek out any number of adult education courses, including real estate and finance. She, not dad, handled the family finances. In this way mother deviated from the 1940s and 50s portrait of the housewife. She would give me a number of biographies to read about women who had succeeded as professionals. These stories afforded me my virtual role models to consider as I approached my college days.

In 1959, I made the decision to start college at San Diego State University. This decision was the result of two major life circumstances. The first was that my parents had no knowledge of the American way of preparing a child to compete for college scholarships. Even if they had, they did not have the financial resources to encourage me to seek admission to an elite private school. The second impetus was that I had become engaged near the end of my senior year in high school to a fellow who was a sophomore at San Diego State University. My parents were close to horrified at my choice of a lower-class guy who lived with his mother and brother in a small trailer. I found him attractive because he was good-looking, fun, older, and an English major who loved baseball as much as I did. I address my undergraduate and graduate school days in the following chapter.

Chapter 6

From Undergraduate to Graduate School:
Years of Growth and Struggle

I attended San Diego State University from 1959 to 1962 and transferred to the University of Washington for my senior year of undergraduate education. I graduated with a bachelor's degree in sociology in 1963. For reasons that I will explain as the story of those years unfolds, I went on to graduate school at the University of Washington, receiving my PhD in sociology at the age of twenty-six in June 1968.

My introduction to life at San Diego State included invitations to join several sororities. I guess my having been an honors student and a student body officer put me on their radar. The independent cuss persona that I had developed in my childhood years led me to find this prospect almost laughable. I went to one sorority rush occasion and that was enough. All the young women I met looked alike and expressed allegiance to their credos of sisterhood—credos that didn't seem to fit me.

I lived at home for my freshman year, commuting with my then fiancé. A major reason for living at home was my mother's psychological state—what was at the time called a nervous breakdown. As the oldest child living at home until my older sister returned mid-year, I was needed to monitor and support my mother. Mother's psychiatrist would not let her talk or engage her in conversation, preferring to send my mom off to have seventeen electric shock treatments. Shock treatments in that day (1959) were far more horrid than what I understand them to be today.

This nightmarish experience led to my having a deep distrust of psychiatry and pretty well ensured that I would not major in psychology.

I did not know what I wanted to major in, but I did know what other majors I did not want, namely education or nursing. Given my childhood years, it may not be surprising that I did not want a nine-to-five job, nor one that was considered a job for females and all that went with that designation. In my first year of exploring career possibilities, no clear option emerged. I found myself attracted to English and French literature and history. Both of those attractions got dashed early on.

Having been an honors student in high school, I was dumfounded by receiving a D on my first essay in an English class. I went right away to meet with the professor. He told me in no uncertain terms that I had a lot to learn about writing a coherent analytical essay. He was right, and I ended up learning a lot from this professor, who put me on a life long journey to become a better writer. This experience also taught me that receiving constructive negative feedback was a gift. This and subsequent experiences of well-considered negative feedback ended up affecting my student mentoring style.

My explorations into French literature and history were satisfying until I realized that I would have to become fluent in the French language. In high school I had studied Spanish and had gotten to the point where I could handle low-level reading comprehension and conversation. Unfortunately, this learning carried over to my attempts to learn to read and speak French. My French language professor called me into his office, due to his exasperation at not knowing how to grade my written work. He said that he did not know if he should grade me on my French or Spanish. Without realizing it, I had written my essays half in Spanish and half in French. While this was funny in an odd way, it also ended my hopes of majoring in French.

I then considered pre-med as a major. Women doctors were virtual role models, due to my mother giving me biographies about them. In my parents' social network, there were a couple of women doctors whose lives seemed to me to be out of balance when it came to the professional and familial sides of their lives. In the late 1950s and early 1960s there was little cultural or structural facilitation of women combining both professional and familial life. I am not so sure that the situation has changed markedly today—maybe a bit culturally, but not structurally. When push came to shove, I rejected pre-med, as I did want to have both a professional and a family life.

When I entered my sophomore year, my college life changed dramatically. My parents decided to move to Seattle, because my dad had accepted a job there as an executive at the Boeing Company. They gave me an ultimatum: I either move with them (in the hope that this would break up my engagement) or I pay most of my own way to remain at San Diego State University. I chose to remain. Not having any savings, I took on three jobs to cover my room and board. I became a resident assistant in the dormitory where I lived, a worker in the student cafeteria, and a marker in a department store, stapling those old-time price labels on articles of clothing.

Living in the dorm and working these jobs opened whole new worlds of friends and experiences. What my parents couldn't do came about naturally, as I became attracted to other fellows and broke off my engagement mid-year. That break up was so painful that it taught me to never again accept an engagement ring, even as I contemplated marriage with a string of other men that I did not end up marrying. I came to understand that even wonderful guys allowed me to explore parts of myself, but I would end up feeling stifled because other parts of me were not fulfilled.

Of my work experiences, I learned a lot about lousy working conditions and the way that payment structures could pit worker against worker. For my cafeteria job, I had to get up and punch the clock by 4:30 a.m. I witnessed what it was like to have a virtual tyrant as a boss. This opened my eyes to what it was like for the full-time workers who depended on that job for their livelihoods. A number of these workers were working-class women of color. As a student worker, I could quit at any time, and I did after the boss went too far. She yelled and almost hit me for screwing up my lettuce cutting. In the department store where I worked, markers earned $1.05 an hour while the salespeople on the floor earned $1.02 an hour. I'll never forget the enmity expressed to me as a marker over this ridiculous difference when we were all underpaid for our labor.

With these experiences under my belt, it makes sense that I began to consider sociology as a major. I was learning a tiny bit of what it was like to be working class. This prompted me to see how my status as a middle-class person gave me the privilege of an imagined future self, not having to suffer the work conditions of the working class, particularly those of color. Thus, for the remainder of my sophomore and junior years, I focused on taking sociology classes. The classes interested me because many of them dealt with the race and class issues that I had become sensitized to in my childhood and work experiences. They also made sense to me, as the sociological perspective forces a multilevel ecological analysis in which the social psychological is contextualized in community and societal conditions. The Chicago School of Sociology and its early twentieth century urban focus with a post-World War II symbolic interactionist approach was particularly attractive to me. I learned from their urban focus on immigrants, gangs, and greater attention to race/class segregation than was customary at the time. I did, however, have an early felt difficulty with either the absence of serious attention to gender, or the warped traditional view of women as socio-emotional actors lacking the task orientation of men.

I got to know my professors—all male—by becoming a reader, grading exams and such for some of the sociology classes. As fate would have it, three of those professors had received their PhDs in sociology from the University of Washington (UW). I knew that UW's sociology department was rated quite highly in the field. These professors encouraged me to go to graduate school pursuing sociology and, of course, at UW. These encouragements and the high rating of the department prompted me to transfer to UW for my senior year, to test out whether I wanted to apply for graduate school there.

I could not afford campus housing or an apartment near campus, so I happily moved in with my parents, who lived in the outskirts of Seattle. I took both undergraduate and graduate sociology courses, and did well in both. I liked my professors and found their courses stimulating, so I was inclined to apply for graduate school at UW. The sociology department had secured a National Institute of Mental Health (NIMH) fellows graduate training grant that would provide financial support for ten or so fellows. Given my performance, a number of professors assured me that I was a shoo-in to receive one of those grants if I applied to their program. Silly me, I believed them. I was mortified when the list of fellows was announced—and fellows they were: all the successful applicants were men. After vociferous confrontations with those professors who had led me down the garden path, I became a "fellow." My suspicion is that a male dropped out, and I was substituted into his place. This incident would turn out to be only the precursor of the sexism that I would experience in my graduate school days.

By sharing expenses with a roommate and having a meager income from the NIMH grant, I was able to move out of my parents' home to an apartment within walking distance of the UW. I loved the beauty of UW campus being situated on the shores of Lake Washington. My apartment was also well situated near the waters of the Montlake canal, where all kinds of boats would pass by. The UW arboretum was a treasure where I spent many hours, even writing my master's thesis there.

These treasures of nature were not matched by my reception into the culture of the sociology department. During the first week of graduate school, I was called into the office of the head of department. At the time (1963), "the head" had greater powers than what we later called department chairs. For example, the head controlled who was recommended for what job. Students could not apply. This fact would later come to affect me directly, as will be unfolded as I move through my graduate school experiences. Being aware of the head's power, I was nervous as I entered his office. He was a distinguished sociologist and, in most ways, a lovely man. He began the conversation by asking how I was doing, but quickly moved to tell me that his department did not discriminate against women. I'm sure that he knew about the ruckus that I had caused over initially being denied a NIMH fellowship. Coming on top of that event, his assurances of no discrimination against women only deepened my understanding that such discrimination was the norm. The word *sexism* was not in vogue at the time.

I began to look into the history of the department regarding the presence of women on the faculty by asking professors and senior-level students. I learned that there had never been a woman on the tenure-track faculty. To my knowledge, the only woman came as a visiting professor for one year. The absence of women faculty continued throughout my graduate school days, leaving me without a female role model.

I became further sensitized to the departmental composition of the graduate student population around me. In conversations with the women, two especially disturbing facts emerged. I was the youngest female student by seven years, and I estimated that half of the women in the program were not in graduate school to go on to academic careers; rather, they were nurses seeking a PhD to become research directors in the healthcare system. These observations motivated me to become a better student than my male colleagues in the same way that people marginalized by race and or other characteristics have done for centuries.

Past experiences were suddenly crystalized into an awareness that this White, middle-class, blond, blue-eyed young woman was an "other." From my childhood days onward, I was aware of my race and class privilege. In graduate school, my sense of lacking gender privilege became acute. Being White and middle class was not sufficient privilege for me to experience equality with males in the struggle to gain a foothold in my endeavors to be recognized as a potentially successful sociologist. Only in later years did I come to articulate my situation at the time as a play on the intersectionality of race, class, and gender.

There were no Black graduate students in the department. (They would have had a much more onerous othering.) There was one Latino male and several Asian-origin students. One, a Japanese American, was the next youngest female student. She became and remains my best friend. Arline had been incarcerated between the ages of seven and twelve in the WWII concentration camps. From her I learned a great deal about how American citizens could be summarily torn from their lives and imprisoned. I also learned how trauma remains, while remarkable resilience unfolds. Arline taught me a term, endure, that helps me to this day to recoup from personal and professional traumas.

The UW sociology department at that time had but two funded research projects: one in demography and the other in organizational sociology. To the best of my recall, neither was funded by a federal agency, so that kind of grant-writing learning opportunity was not available to students. In any case, I wasn't interested in either project. Students with interests like mine had to create their own project ideas and proceed to design and implement research pretty much on their own. Close mentorship of the kind I would come to value in my future interactions with advisees was not the norm. The upside of this culture was that we learned by doing.

As it came time to select a master's thesis topic, I choose to examine how leaders emerge around the context of an issue, rather than leaders being leaders across all issues. This hypothesis was provoked by my learning about the classic great man versus situational context debate in social history. I approached my favorite social psychology professor to ask him to be the chair of my master's committee. His response was memorable. He asked, "Why should I take on this project when all you are going to do is get married and have children?" The obvious implication was that

I would choose to give up hopes of being a professional and take on the traditional female role. My naïve response was, "But you are married and have children." To which he responded that that was different. In the end, he reluctantly agreed to serve as chair and did a pretty good job. This experience deepened my understanding that I was not perceived as a student who would add luster to the reputation of a professor or my school.

The positivist orientation of the department (radical empiricism) meant that we did primarily quantitative research, spending a great deal of time collecting and analyzing our own data. For my master's thesis, I collected a large survey data set involving students in several high schools. These were the early days of huge computers fed by punch cards. With the help of more senior students, I was able to conduct sociometric analyses (students' selection of opinion leaders over a variety of issues) that led to support of my hypothesis. The research was never published, largely because there was neither the expectation nor facilitation of graduate students learning how to write a journal article.

The initial visibility of the department was established in 1945, when the renowned logical positivist George Lundberg joined the UW faculty. Professor Lundberg had retired in 1963, but his influence was still evident during my graduate school days. The graduate students got to know Professor Lundberg as a lovely man who came to our basement quarters often. When we realized that he did not have an office post-retirement, we gave up one of the fellows' offices for him to use and made it as nice as we could.

Despite our fondness for Professor Lundberg, my cohort had many debates about the tenets of logical positivism. I learned a great deal from fellow graduate students through these debates and from their recommendations to read scholars who challenged the premise that the research methods of physics could be wholly adopted by the social sciences. In other words, we read scholars who rejected the idea that studying people was the same as studying a physical phenomenon. Such scholars were not given prominence in our course reading lists. For example, Max Weber was given short shrift in my theory course, being characterized as a subjectivist as opposed to the objectivist positioning of positivism. Of the nineteenth- and twentieth-century classical scholars, my outside-of-class reading included Max Weber, Robert Park, Herbert Blumer, Morris Janowitz, Charles Wright, C. Wright Mills, Berger and Luckmann, Theodor Adorno, and Alvin Gouldner.

In general, these readings moved me to incorporate into my theorizing the concepts of power, conflict, social construction of reality, legitimacy as the basis of authority, a commitment to social change, and media as a major social force. My notions of appropriate methodologies expanded to include interpretative and qualitative methods. I also had to negotiate the pluses and minuses of the dominant structural functionalist orientation of Talcott Parsons taught in my classroom. That orientation, with its emphasis upon socializing people into value and normative consensus in the service of social controls that efficiently undergirded and legitimated a stratified society, clashed with the way of thinking I encountered outside the classroom.

When it came time for me to formulate a doctoral dissertation project, I was taken with John Dewey's concept of felt difficulty and Tamotsu Shibutani's concept of ambiguity as unfolded in his 1966 book, *Improvised News: A Sociological Study of Rumor*. Felt difficulty resonated with me partly because it captured my own experience of how formal and informal education provoked a reconsideration of what I thought I knew. Á la Dewey, felt difficulty with one's beliefs opened the door to learning that could change your understandings of the social world.

Shibutani's book changed my understanding of rumor. I had been taught the serial transmission model of rumor, wherein the initial story was changed through omission and addition of facts as the story went from one person to the next. Shibutani was one of a very few scholars who conceptualized ambiguity. He centered it in his study of how the Japanese experiencing the atomic bomb collectively made sense of a phenomenon for which they had no prior experience. In this way, his work was more than a study of rumor. It was a symbolic interactionist and pragmatist theory of how people co-construct a social reality of ambiguous phenomena.

Adorno's concept of structural ambiguity also came into play indirectly insofar as it addressed how the larger societal structure could create ambiguity by inconsistencies between the normative and the actual behavioral world. One final premise in the literature that led to my focus on ambiguity as the central concept in my doctoral dissertation came from some collective behavior scholars. They argued that collectives experiencing intense ambiguity would often act irrationally, even hysterically. With the influence of Shibutani on my thinking, I sought to conduct research that would counter this argument.

Being inclined toward theory, I explicated a concept of ambiguity. I identified two types, pervasive and focused. Pervasive ambiguity occurs when people are unable to determine the relational links between themselves and other elements in the social environment and are, therefore, unable to identify the contextual meaning of the situation. This leaves people with no direct way of knowing how they could or should interact with others or the environment, and thus the capacity to engage in meaningful social action is impaired. Put briefly, there is insufficient information to construct a definition of the situation or to choose between alternative definitions. As a result, the experience of ambiguity goes beyond a lack of information to also become an affective problem of stress when one's ability to make sense of the world is threatened. Focused ambiguity is more straightforward. It occurs when people have a definition of the situation but are unable to determine an appropriate strategy of action to deal with the known contingencies of the situation. For example, persons who don't know or cannot decide how to attain a goal are experiencing ambiguity that is focused upon finding a means to desired ends.

For my dissertation research, I decided to focus on the more unsettling problem of pervasive ambiguity. In large part, this decision was due to what I saw as the phenomenological reality or lived experience of pervasive ambiguity in the 1960s. This was a time marked by both social conflict and social change generated by political assassinations, the Vietnam War, and the civil rights movement. As I experience the world around me today, I think that by studying ambiguity, I was doomed to live it thereafter.

Of the various hypotheses I proposed, the most important was overt consensual acceptance of a proposed definition of the situation is prerequisite to ambiguity resolution. The challenge became the development of a research design that created the conditions of pervasive ambiguity. The design I created was, to say the least, unconventional. Because it involved deception and a lack of informed consent, it would not pass muster with the institutional review boards that developed well after my doctoral student days.

I turned a small groups laboratory with its one-way mirror into a space void of environmental clues to as to what was going on. The lab was in a basement with no windows. From a survey of students in multiple summer school classes, I was able to select participants who had no prior experience with experiments and were strangers to one another. The invitation to participate created the expectation that they were going to participate in an hour-long supervised experiment for which they would receive course credit. Six sessions of varying composition regarding age and gender were created. When participants arrived at the small groups lab, no one was there to meet them. They entered a room with no furniture and with a generous amount of dirt on the floor. The dirt was there because, in pre-tests, participants sat down on their coats or books, thereby defeating my need to observe their patterns of interaction and action. All in all, this situation met the conditions of pervasive ambiguity. The participants had no way to figure out their relationship to the environment or to the other strangers in the room, or to know what was going on—to define the situation.

There were travel posters on each wall, behind which were sensitive microphones recording participants' verbal interactions. Behind the one-way mirror was a videotaping machine that provided data about participants' actions. If a participant went out into the hallway to inquire, my collaborators were trained to say that they did not know where the experimenter was or what was going on. My dissertation chair, Otto Larsen, and other committee members were convinced that I would not collect the data I needed because no one would put up with the truly uncomfortable conditions of the room and the absence of any way to verify that they were in the right place for the anticipated experiment. I disagreed, due to the belief that pervasive ambiguity presents a felt difficulty that needs to be resolved. Of the eighty-nine participants, only three ended up escaping by leaving the building. I had a person posted at the building exit to ask them to go to the debriefing room, where I would meet with them.

The first problem participants faced was to collectively decide if "this" was the experiment. There was a cyclical pattern of information seeking and tension release. For example, it was common for participants to talk with each other to see if they had anything in common that might explain why these strangers had been brought together, followed by conversations about anything but the ambiguity (e.g., movies, hair styles, or their favorite classes). Once they decided that "this" was the experiment, participants went on to throw out hypotheses about what the experiment "was." Hypotheses varied from paranoid suggestions that there were electrical forces under the floor that would force all of them into one corner, to the idea that the experimenter wanted to observe leadership development. If their information-seeking led to no consensus, they would move on to tension release or another hypothesis. The funniest of them all emerged when a young man noticed a Marlboro cigarette box in the middle of the floor and exclaimed "that's it—there is a recording device in that box!" All participants circled the box, and the fellow stomped the heck out of it. My helpers had neglected to remove it after the prior session. When no recording device was found, they all laughed and released some tension.

To my surprise, two of the sessions reached consensus on the correct hypothesis; namely, that the experiment was about how people come together to make sense of an ambiguous situation. A questionnaire administered immediately after I came in to end the session confirmed that all the individuals in these sessions had adopted the consensual hypothesis. Participants in the remaining four sessions were either still hypothesizing or said they were waiting for an explanation when the session time was over. Despite the discomfort of the situation, the participants endured. Most indicated in their questionnaire responses that they felt they had an interesting experience and were not angry. One reason for the lack of anger was that they got to meet new people and now had a basis of possible friendship from having had a shared experience.

All in all, this experience taught me that I could successfully challenge authority and trust my intuitions. My professors were wrong in their prediction that I would fail to pull the study off. I came away with some understanding of the power of pervasive ambiguity and the heavy requirements of its resolution. The lack of consensus in the world around me today pulls me back to this dissertation research with considerable trepidation.

Unfortunately, analysis of my dissertation data did not happen during my tenure at UW, because I got peritonitis in the spring of 1967. It took several months for me to recover. Because my NIMH grant funding was coming to an end after four years, I had to find a job. I knew I wanted to become an academic, in large part because I valued the autonomy of that life and career style. Despite the fact that Arline and I were at the top of our cohort performance-wise, the department head, with his control over who was put forth for open assistant professor positions, only recommended men. Quite by chance, Professor Gordon Hirabayashi, an alumnus of the UW sociology PhD program, was visiting my advisor, Otto Larsen. He was looking for someone who could join his faculty to teach quantitative methods at University of Alberta in Edmonton, Canada. This is the same Gordon Hirabayashi who gained fame for his Supreme Court fight against the internment of Japanese Americans and for his opposition to war as a Quaker conscientious objector. We met, and he was willing to hire me ABD (all but dissertation) starting in the fall of 1967. As I had no other job possibilities and liked Hirabayashi and the idea of returning to my Canadian place of birth, I accepted the job. Moving to Edmonton, which seemed like the last stop to the North Pole with its seven months of snow and ice, led to some hilarious experiences. I will unfold these as I move to the next chapter to summarize the turbulent times of my early career.

Chapter 7

From Place to Place
at Quite a Pace

My fifty-three-year career began as an assistant professor of sociology at the University of Alberta (1967–69) during which time I completed my PhD in June 1968. The university graciously granted me leave from August 1968 to the spring of 1969 to join the staff of the National Commission on the Causes and Prevention of Violence as co-director of the Media and Violence Task Force. I detail my journeys to three other institutions in a five-year period as I move through this chapter.

My move to Edmonton, Alberta, was memorable. It began with my parents and me driving to the Canadian border. The border control agent wanted to know if I could support myself, so he asked me how much money I had. I responded that I had ninety-nine cents in my pocket. My parents bellowed, "Tell him that you have a job at the university!" We all laughed heartily and entered Canada.

When we got to Edmonton, I wanted to fulfill my promise to myself that when I got my first job, I would buy a sports car. I bought a Triumph GT6. That fateful act came back to bite me when winter came with snow, ice, and wind for more than seven months. I had bought a car completely unsuited for those conditions. I could not navigate the roads without fishtailing when I hit the ice. I ended up putting sandbags in the trunk of my car and often asked the heaviest colleague to drive with me to events!

My reception by my departmental colleagues was more comforting than my driving experiences. My department chair Gordon Hirabayashi and his then wife, Esther, were especially gracious and helpful. Coming from California and Seattle, I had no idea of what it was like to live in the winter conditions of Edmonton. Expecting that I did not have the right clothing, Esther took me shopping at Hudson's department store. She kindly guided me to buy a massive fur coat and heavy-duty boots. Those boots unfortunately had leather heels that did not do well on the ice. On my first entry into my campus building, I hit the ice at the entry and slid on my backside all the way to the elevator.

My first class as an assistant professor was equally memorable. I was hired to teach research methods, so my first class was a statistics course. I walked nervously to the classroom, but couldn't find it, as the classroom numbers were not consecutively laid out. By the time I found the right classroom, I was even more shaken up. I started to write the name of the class and my name on the blackboard. In Canada at that time, students stood up when a professor entered the classroom. The 250 students, both undergraduate and graduate, did not stand up. A fellow yelled out, "Ah come on, sit down until the professor arrives!" I meekly responded, "I am the professor." Many of the students were older than my twenty-six years. After that clumsy beginning, the class ended up going well.

I enjoyed my time in Edmonton. At that time, it was almost like a frontier town with a multiethnic population. The sociology department at the University of Alberta was young and rapidly growing in the size of its faculty and the nascent doctoral program. As I recall, I was one of two women on the faculty. The only non-White faculty members were the Japanese American chair and the Palestinian Canadian associate chair. Partly because I was from the respected University of Washington and had research credentials, I did not experience much in the way of discrimination. My being White and having the cultural capital of being middle class obviously helped. It also did not hurt that I had a good relationship with the Hirabayashis and became good friends with the associate department chair Baha Abu-Leban and his wife, Sharon.

Another plus of living in Edmonton was that I got to experience my Canadian birthplace. While Edmonton was vastly different from my birthplace in Ottawa, I still got to learn much about the political and cultural differences between Canada and the United States. I loved the Canadian universal healthcare system, and even learned a bit about hockey. It was surprising to me that Vietnam War protests were quite active on campus.

They were led in part by my political scientist friend and American expat, Christian Bay. I joined these protests and did not suffer any negative reactions. Of course, Canadian forces were participants in the war, but the focus of the protests was directed at the United States. My Canadian friends observed that Canadians were not inclined to protest their own government's policies but loved to protest against the United States.

As previously noted, my doctoral advisor, Otto Larsen, played a role in my getting a position at the University of Alberta, and he was also instrumental in my joining the staff of the Violence Commission as co-director of the Media and Violence Task Force. I had gained expertise in the area of media effects largely through Otto's classes. He was offered the co-director position and turned it down, with the suggestion that they offer the position to me. During the 1968 protests focused on the Vietnam War and the Civil Rights Movement many of my friends were so convinced that change was not possible by working within the system, that they fled to Canada or adopted Timothy Leary's philosophy of dropping out through using LSD and other psychedelics. For my part, I did not use drugs and held on to the belief that change was possible by working within the system. I was profoundly affected not only by the assassinations of Martin Luther King Jr., Medgar Evers, Malcolm X, and too many others, but also most directly by the assassination of Robert Kennedy in June 1968. This was the same month that I came back to Seattle for my dissertation oral exam and successfully completing my PhD. Robert Kennedy's assassination created a felt difficulty in me. If I believed change was possible within the system, then it was time to put my money where my mouth was and accept the Violence Commission position as co-director of the Media and Violence Task Force. I remain grateful to my University of Alberta colleagues for granting me leave, even though it was only the fall semester of my second year at the university.

President Lyndon B. Johnson created the Violence Commission in response to Robert Kennedy's assassination, and appointed Milton Eisenhower, brother of Dwight, as its head. The scuttlebutt was that President Johnson told a staff member to get Eisenhower, and the staff member called Milton, rather than Johnson's wish to enlist former president Dwight D. Eisenhower. That mistake, if it was really a mistake, proved fortuitous. Milton had been the president of three universities including Johns Hopkins and had extensive high-level government experience.

For the first and I believe the only time, the commission staff featured academics living in residence in Washington, DC, as partners with the usual crew of lawyers. The lawyers ranged from Justice Department youngsters to powerful law firm attorneys with insider status in government. The command staff included two sociologists (Jim Short and Marvin Wolfgang) as research directors. There were a number of task forces, each with a lawyer and an academic as co-directors. This composition differed dramatically from the usual role of academics as consultants who would periodically come into town to meet with commission staff. This is not to say that academics had equal power. The chief of staff was Lloyd Cutler, whom Stuart Taylor in the May 2005 issue of *The Atlantic* called "The Last Super Lawyer." Cutler was a partner in a prominent law firm and played major roles in national and international politics, including serving as the White House Counsel in both Jimmy Carter's and Bill Clinton's administrations.

The commissioners were an amazing mix of insiders, such as Senator Philip Hart, Leon Jaworski (renowned lawyer and LBJ advisor), Congressman Hale Boggs, and Terrance Cardinal Cook. The social scientist representative, Eric Hoffer, was downright hysterical. While Hoffer was rightly credited as a moral and social philosopher, he evidenced disdain for academics. He prided himself in never having gone to school, and his most prized identity was as a longshoreman on the San Francisco docks. Hoffer taunted the social scientists who testified at commission public hearings. The most common event was him slamming the desk and shouting something like, "Give me a 'yes' or 'no' answer and none of your 'it depends' qualifications about your research findings!"

There were many reasons for the high-profile composition of commissioners, but the most relevant for my role as co-director of the Media and Violence Task Force was that Lyndon Johnson and his wife Lady Bird owned a number of media organizations. A well-known columnist of the time, Drew Pearson of the *Washington Post*, wrote a column suggesting that my task force would whitewash the role of the media in causing violence. He also directly attacked me as a foreigner who knew nothing about the American media—evidently due to my birth in Canada. This was shabby reporting. I had left Canada for the United States as a ten-month-old infant. Nonetheless, his column put a spotlight on my task force that led to an attempt by the Johnson administration to interfere with our task force findings.

I was a brand-new PhD with no experience in governmental politics, much less national politics. Not only that, but I was also the only woman among a fifty-person all-White professional staff, and the youngest member by far! My co-director, Robert Baker, was a lawyer in the Department of Justice. At our first meeting, he said that we could start writing the report right away. I was aghast. I responded as a social scientist and said, "No, we have to do research and bring in the most prominent experts on the question of whether the media causes violence." In essence, we were dealing with the epistemological differences between a lawyer starting with a conclusion and building a case, and a social scientist well versed in the controversies surrounding the question. As such, my position was that we had to give equal voice to experts with differing perspectives and we needed to add to the literature by conducting new research.

The lawyer/social scientist contestation pervaded the whole commission enterprise. With the help of the research directors, and Jim Short in particular, the social scientists in other task forces and I mostly got to do things our way. For example, my task force conducted a national survey and held a memorable public hearing with the best experts in the field. The media always pays attention to any event concerning its interests, especially given the prior purported assertion that my task force would protect the interests of President Johnson. Eric Hoffer did his thing, but each of the male experts held his own. The staff sat around the walls of the hearing room, and I was the only woman among them. A commissioner approached me and asked that I make a Xerox copy of something for him. I had the gumption to say that I was not a secretary, but co-director of the task force. He demurred.

The commission staff was located in the new Executive Office Building close to Lafayette Park, where there were frequent demonstrations against the Vietnam War met by police in riot gear. The commission worked in the larger context of national upheaval, including the protests at the 1968 Democratic Party National Convention that a commission's task force (*The Walker Report*) labeled a police riot. With the upheavals and the sensitivity of the Violence Commission's work, there was a heavy emphasis on security along with careful FBI assessments of each staff member and all outside experts that we wanted to engage. When we got into an elevator, we were told not to talk. I saw this as a funny way to make us feel that what we had to say was important. All documents had to be put in a secure file at the end of long working days.

The FBI challenged 40 percent of the experts or consultants that I wanted to engage. Their "red files" suggested these individuals were suspect. I found out that my red file also tagged me as somewhat suspect due to my participation in protests against the Vietnam War and the magazines I subscribed to, such as *Ramparts* and the *I. F. Stone Weekly Newsletter.* I, along with the research directors and other social science co-directors, had to argue long and hard to engage our experts. I don't know if the executive leadership had to argue for me to become a co-director.

On top of all the security provisions, my co-director alerted me to the fact that our phones were being tapped. As I look back, I am amazed by my guts in using the tapped phones to ward off White House attempts to influence the conclusions of our task force report. These consisted of inquiries to the top lawyer staff about what we were going to conclude about media and violence, inquiries passed along to my co-director and from him to me. Increasingly upset by what seemed to be pressure to conclude that the media did not cause violence, I decided to act. I called one of our experts whom I knew professionally, and after chitchat, told him about the pressure and that if it did not stop, I would hold a press conference to expose it. Confirmation that our phones were tapped came quickly. The next day I was informed by my co-director that we were to go to the White House West Wing to meet with the president's chief domestic advisor and cabinet member, Joseph Califano Jr. Even before I could express my concerns at the meeting, Califano proceeded to assure us that there would be no White House interference with our task force.

Before I conclude the highlights of the Violence Commission experience and how it affected me as a researcher/scholar, I should briefly comment on what it was like to be the only woman on a fifty-person professional staff. I think I made it clear early on that I would not take no for an answer. I had the support of Jim Short, one of the research directors, and that was essential in lessening the power of the executive lawyer staff to control my behavior. In contrast to the young lawyers on the staff, those prominent lawyers did not have the power to sabotage my career in the academy. While I did find ways to be regarded as a player, I felt the loneliness of still having no female models from whom I could seek advice. I knew that a well-known woman social psychologist, whose work on media effects I had read, was working as a program officer at one of the federal-funding agencies. I contacted her and made an appointment to meet. That meeting was disappointing at best. Basically, she told me that she made it on her own, and it was up to me to do the same. She was unwilling to discuss, much less acknowledge, sexism.

Nonetheless, my Violence Commission experience was pivotal in setting the stage for my development as a researcher/scholar who would go on to challenge the prevailing theories of media effects and theories of violence. It also turned my focus to the nature of power and seriously undermined my belief that change could be achieved by working within the system. The phenomenological experiences I was observing in the world around me did not jibe with the research-based conclusion that the media had only short-term effects of an increased likelihood of violence and only under certain limited conditions. Nonetheless, that was the conclusion drawn from the research literature and was, therefore, the conclusion reached in our *Media and Violence Task Force Report*, published in 1969.

As a sociologist, I was dissatisfied with the psychological focus on individuals that dominated the research literature on media and violence. That focus was on the message, not on the whole media system and its control over scarce information resources that determined what we could know beyond our immediate life experience. The collective violence that dominated that era—urban uprisings, protests, and inter-group conflicts—was left out of the story. Equally important was the power of the media to frame violence as legitimate or illegitimate. Of course, the media system of that time differed greatly in its centralized structure as opposed to the decentralized structure after the development of cable and the internet-based venues. However, those changes do not really alter the fact that the media not only tell us what is happening, but also frame events as good/bad or legitimate/illegitimate. These felt difficulties with the research literature led me to develop a sociological theory of media effects later in my career.

I came to question not only the prevailing theories of media effects, but also the prevailing theories of violence. Social movements of that time delegitimized the physical force of war and police actions against protestors by labeling them acts of violence. This prompted me to ask a disruptive question: Is the definition of violence as illegal or illegitimate acts of physical force that can cause harm a definition that serves the interests of the power structure? In other words, is violence defined to exclude similar acts of physical force performed by power holders and their institutions? I asked myself: What would be the result of including legal and legitimated acts of harmful physical force in our theories of violence? Put another way: What if we developed theories of violence that included both legitimated violence in the service of social control and delegitimated violence in the service of other goals? This change would disrupt prevailing theories focused upon illegitimate violence understood as the product of lower-class values, machismo, relative deprivation, excessive alcohol intake, aggressive clues (e.g., police in riot gear), and inadequacies in childhood socialization. Suffice it to say that I went on later in my career to develop a conflict theory of violence that focused on asymmetric or unequal power relations as the cause of all violence regardless of its legitimacy status.

All in all, my Violence Commission experience radicalized me in the sense that I came away challenging the conventional ways of understanding both media effects and violence. I also came away with a much more skeptical view of the ability to bring about change by working within the system. A Violence Commission member, Congressman Hale Boggs, approached me at a social event and asked me what I thought would be the impact of my task force report. Without waiting for me to reply, he said that it would gather dust in some archive, suggesting that it would have no effect. He was correct.

Richard Nixon assumed the presidency in January 1969, before the Violence Commission ended in June of that year. One of his first actions was to upstage our task force report by appointing a Surgeon General's Scientific Advisory Committee on Television and Social Behavior. That took the wind out of our sails. This action fit with the long history of governmental investigations of media effects, such as that of Estes Kefauver addressing comic books and juvenile delinquency in 1954. I came to understand that even with Milton Eisenhower's innovation of having academics working in residence and partnership with lawyers, there was no way academics who were not embedded inside the power structure could have more than a tiny and fleeting influence on governmental policy.

In the spring of 1969, I returned to my teaching duties at the University of Alberta and dealt with the challenge of commuting to Washington,

DC, every month to complete my Violence Commission work. One of the benefits of being on the Violence Commission was that it increased my visibility as a researcher/scholar addressing one of the hot issues of the time. I received two job offers, one from the Michigan State University's (MSU) Department of Sociology and the other from the Annenberg School for Communication at the University of Pennsylvania. I opted to take the MSU position, as I was not ready to change my professional identity as a sociologist to join a communication faculty. The MSU sociology department had a good reputation, and I knew the work of some of the MSU professors (e.g., William Form, Joan Huber, John Useem, and Wilbur Brookover). This meant that I said goodbye to my generous University of Alberta colleagues in June 1969.

My tenure as an assistant professor at MSU (1969–72) was complex in both professional and personal ways. I arrived in East Lansing in August 1969. Initially, my colleagues were supportive, and the department was congenial. Of course, White male domination was the order of the day, with only two women on the faculty. The Vietnam War protests dominated the environment in which we worked. As an activist, I participated in the protests, and when a university strike was called, I joined the strike. I wasn't alone, as some of the younger faculty and one older faculty member, John Useem, also joined. The predictable outcome was a rather hostile split among the departmental faculty members. One faculty member actually attacked the faculty strikers, calling us communists.

On the personal front, back when I was on the Violence Commission staff, I had reached out to the best sociologist working on American values, Robin Williams, to ask him to be a consultant. I wanted the media effects literature to consider media effects on the values that legitimated or delegitimated violence. Robin told me that he was overloaded and suggested that the only other person who knew as much about values as he did was the social psychologist Milton Rokeach. I called Professor Rokeach, and he agreed to become a consultant. I met him a couple of times when he was in Washington, DC, for National Science Foundation meetings. We had good conversations, and I liked him. He was in the MSU Department of Psychology.

Shortly after my arrival at MSU, I looked Professor Rokeach up, and we met over lunch and at protest events. It turns out that he had only recently been divorced from his first wife. Despite our significant age

Sandra and Mendel at their wedding reception, 1969.

difference—he being twenty-three years older than I—there was chemistry between us that I had never felt before in the many romances I had had in the past. The sparks were flying, and our relationship developed quickly. I had found the relationship that I had been looking for where I could be all my selves—sexual, playful, intellectual, vulnerable, and adventurous. In contrast to my prior relationships, I never felt loneliness in his presence. We were married in December 1969.

Our marriage was highly visible, as Milton was a star, not only in the field of psychology, but also in his twenty-four-year prominence in the MSU community. For him and for me, the most emotionally complex concerns were the reaction and welfare of his three children and the unavoidable hurt to his highly respected first wife. Suffice it to say that these concerns were central to our married life for many years but were largely resolved by our commitments to work through the challenges and by the children's efforts to adjust to their new family reality. Each child had a different reaction, and only one of them remained angry. Subsequent events that I will address when I get to my later career laid the groundwork for an unusual and meaningful familial bonding that included Milton's first wife.

As for my parents, they said that they did not have any objection to Milton being Jewish but were understandably concerned about our age difference. They still lived in Seattle at the time. They gave us support by holding a wedding reception that a lot of my Seattle friends and even some of my UW professors attended. As time progressed, my parents came to accept and love my husband. My father told me that he understood that my primary attraction to my husband was intellectual. I responded, "Forget the intellectual and go for the adventurous and sexual." My complex and often unhappy relationship with two of my three siblings meant that they were sometimes in and sometimes out of our lives. Any animosity was directed at me, not at Milton.

Milton had a deep cultural identification with being Jewish but was secular (non-observant). Around this time, I acted on my preference for Milton's softer Hebrew name, Mendel, and henceforth I will refer to him as Mendel. Mendel had a rich and significant life history, but this is not the place to go into that, except as it pertains to my career development. With Mendel being a well-known social psychologist considerably older than this young fledgling academic, many people thought that I was his student who would play second fiddle in our relationship. Nothing could have been further from the truth. I insisted on equality in every respect of our relationship. For example, I insisted on paying half of our living expenses despite Mendel's salary being considerably higher than mine.

Mendel had been a serious player in promoting racial equality and the rights of the gay community. Nonetheless, being a man of his generation, he found it difficult to acknowledge sexism. It took many fights between us over the years before he saw the light. One of my first acts was to deviate from what I saw as the sexist practice of wives in the United States taking the husband's last name as theirs. I was one of the early women to deviate from that practice by compromising and going with Ball-Rokeach as my last name.

The turbulent times of my first year at MSU were cut short by two considerations. The first was the difficulty our marriage posed for Mendel's children and his first wife by our living in the same town (East

Sandra and Mendel, 1977.

Lansing). The second was a fortuitous invitation in 1970 from the psychology department at the University of Western Ontario (UWO) for Mendel to join their faculty. Early discussions with the department chair, William McClelland, made it clear that the sociology department would also offer me a position. The end result of the negotiations was that MSU would approve our going on leave for two years, and this was acceptable to the UWO administration.

UWO is located in London, Ontario, a medium-sized city about ninety miles west of Toronto. The psychology department had a faculty with some well-known scholars, while the sociology department was relatively weak, with demography being their focus. Both faculties were all White with no openly gay members.

One memorable classroom experience occurred in October 1970, when I observed another cultural difference between Americans and Canadians. The Separatist FLQ (Front de Liberation du Quebec) kidnapped two of President Pierre Trudeau's cabinet members and killed one of them. This event followed several violent protests aimed at the separation of the French-speaking Quebec from the rest of English-speaking Canada. In response to the kidnappings, President Trudeau declared the War Measures Act, suspending civil rights throughout Canada. In the classroom, I asked students how they felt about losing their civil rights. In contrast to my alarm as an American, the Canadian students were quite accepting. From their point of view, only the Quebecois were at risk.

I liked the people in my department, but we did not have much in common in terms of our research interests. As a result, this was not the place where I could thrive professionally. Nonetheless, Mendel and I loved our time in London. We were welcomed with open arms by the psychology faculty and beyond to fellow travelers who loved music, theater, and fishing. We developed a lifelong friendship with the McClellands. William (or Bill as he was known), was chair of the psychology department. His spouse, Marilyn, was a clinical psychologist working in a hospital and with the local schools to diagnose early childhood learning and other disabilities. They invited us to stay at their cottage in Georgian Bay, on an island seven miles by boat from Parry Sound. You wouldn't have thought that Mendel, a Jewish boy from Brooklyn, would not only take to fishing, but also become almost obsessed with it. Fortunately, I loved the mystery of casting a line and trying to imagine what was going on in the waters below. Georgian Bay was a wonderland of natural beauty full of stunning flora and fauna. For thirteen summers thereafter, we would return to Georgian Bay, renting a cottage on an island next to the McClellands. All in all, our two-year experience in London gave us the warm space to build our marriage.

We were torn when, early in 1972, a new opportunity for positions at Washington State University (WSU) came into play. I loved living a very different aspect of Canadian culture from what I experienced in Edmonton, but from my point of view, there was little career advantage in staying at UWO. Both of us were hesitant to return to MSU for the same personal reasons that led us to leave East Lansing. I had several reasons to be attracted to the idea of accepting positions at WSU. A major one was that by going to the University of Alberta, then to the Violence Commission, then to MSU, and then to UWO, I had little to show by way of publications beyond the *Media and Violence Task Force Report*. In those five years, I had taught eleven different courses, requiring a great deal of preparation. Going to a strong sociology department might give me the time and working conditions to concentrate on turning my questioning of established theories into my own research program to test and publish alternative theories.

The opening inquiry from WSU came from the sociology department chair, Melvin DeFleur, who was an admirer of Mendel's work. At the same time, there was interest in me emanating from Jim Short, the research co-director of the Violence Commission. Jim had invited me to write a chapter in a book he was co-editing entitled *Collective Violence*. My chapter, "The Legitimation of Violence," was published in the volume in 1972. The sociology department at WSU was highly rated, so even though we would be moving to a small college town (Pullman), the move looked like a good opportunity career-wise, especially for me. The first five stimulating but chaotic years of my career covered in this chapter were followed by fourteen years at WSU, where my career aspirations began to be fulfilled.

Sandra and Mendel fishing on Georgian Bay, circa 1971.

Chapter 8

Growing and Challenging Years:
Washington State University

Washington State University (WSU) is located in Pullman, a small town in the Palouse country of the southeast corner of Washington state. Pullman is a university town located in an extremely conservative rural area, where the primary economy rested on the growing of wheat and lentils. The rolling hills have a distinctive beauty, alight with waving fields of wheat. When we arrived in the summer of 1972, the resident population was about eight thousand and the student population approximately fifteen thousand.

Neither Mendel nor I had ever lived in a small town. We would come to learn a lot about small-town life, most of it charming and supportive. Of course, there were disturbing surprises. Driving into Pullman for the first time, we stopped at a Chinese restaurant in nearby Colfax and ordered chicken chow mein. It arrived with some sort of gravy spread generously over it! Good restaurants were not abundant. We were also taken aback at first by the loss of anonymity. It seemed that everyone knew who you were, whether it be at the bank, other businesses, or public places. One incident I will never forget was when my late good friend, Julie Lutz (a WSU astronomer and later an associate provost), and I wanted to get our ears pierced. We were both in our early forties, and the only doctor in town who did ear piercing was an obstetrician. So we went to his office full of pregnant women and got our ears done. The rumor that went around town in a flash was that Julie and I were pregnant.

My fourteen years in the WSU sociology department (1972–86) were years of professional growth and personal happiness, despite a number of medical challenges that emerged for both Mendel and me. We considered Pullman an oasis where we had the time and the support to do our work with a treasure chest of friends. We traveled often, nationally and internationally, which offset the downsides of small town isolation.

The sociology department and the university were unique in a number of ways. While the sociology department had a very good reputation with some excellent scholars, it was difficult to attract faculty to come and to stay in "the boonies" of Pullman. Jim Short was an exception. After finishing his PhD at the University of Chicago, he spent his entire career from 1951 until his retirement in 1997 at WSU. Jim was a well-known academic and a major contributor to the national and international worlds of sociology.

Another major player in building the department was Wallis Beasley. Wallis had gone on to become university provost and was the provost when we arrived. It was most unusual for a social scientist to sit in such a high university position. Also unusual was the fact that the university president, Glenn Terrell, was a psychologist. These two administrators, and especially Wallis Beasley, became important supporters of our work.

When Melvin DeFleur became chair of the sociology department, he and his sociologist spouse, Lois DeFleur, talked with a receptive administration about a strategy of hiring professional couples to offset the difficulty of attracting scholars to Pullman. Most universities at the time still refused to hire professional couples due to the long-standing assumption of nepotism or the idea that the more powerful spouse would favor the other. Lois DeFleur tells her own story in this volume, but the idea that she would be favored was clearly wrong. She joined the sociology department in 1967 with a one-sixteenth appointment in sociology and the rest of her appointment in the Department of Rural Sociology in the College of Agriculture. So, nepotism thinking and sexism still came into play in the late 60s. That is probably one reason why Lois had a great deal to do with the idea of hiring professional couples as equals in the 1970s WSU Department of Sociology.

In addition to being ahead of other universities with respect to hiring couples, the WSU sociology department made concerted efforts to recruit faculty and students of color. Under the leadership of Wallis Beasley and

Jim Short, these efforts were initiated well before diversity requirements came into play. Recruitment of such faculty were not successful, due in large part to the remoteness of Pullman and its lack of resident communities of color. Once faculty diversity requirements emerged, WSU could not compete with elite institutions or with institutions located in areas with established communities of color. These efforts were successful in recruiting some Black male graduate students, however. William Julius Wilson was one of these students earning his PhD in 1966. He went on to become a famous sociologist.

I had a full-time position in the sociology department. With Mendel being a psychologist, the arrangement was that he would have a quarter-time appointment in the Department of Psychology and a three-fourths appointment in sociology. This arrangement proved propitious. The psychology department had little in the way of his specialty, social psychology, and was not as strong as the sociology department. The collegiality of the sociology department extended to the both of us. When a faculty member, Victor Gecas, found out that Mendel was an ardent and spunky handball player, they set up regular play times. When other colleagues discovered that Mendel loved poker, he was brought into their poker-playing group. These inclusions meant that not only was Mendel a highly respected academic, but also his being in a sociology department was not at all alienating.

Lois had broken the glass ceiling for me in 1969. She was the first women to hold a full-time faculty position in the WSU sociology department. I was once again one of two women in the department. The faculty was all White. My race and class privilege gave me important access to a faculty position. I do not recall experiencing much in the way of overt sexism in my department. One male faculty member did go ballistic in a faculty meeting when I was arguing for affirmative action. He mistook it as a personal attack. Fortunately, the rest of the faculty convinced him that I had not attacked him. As I look back, I think my presentation of self along with the liberal politics of most, but not all, of the faculty may have reduced expressions of sexism. I think of a remark made to me by a senior faculty member and close friend, Irving Tallman, who said he loved my irreverence. It probably also helped that I did not always agree with Mendel's position on an issues discussed in faculty meetings. Later, when I was more involved in the larger university community, I would come to experience resistance to efforts to address sexism on campus.

I was glad to be at a land-grant state university. WSU was a markedly different campus from that of the University of Washington where I did my graduate work. The WSU campus was much smaller and cozier. The sociology department was located in Wilson Hall, subsequently renamed Wilson-Short Hall in honor of Jim Short. It did not take long to go from our building to the bookstore or even the football stadium, where my husband and I ran around the track for exercise.

I loved the mix of the student body coming from different backgrounds and social classes. Of course, at that time and given the location of Pullman, most of the students were White, but there were rural/urban and class variations. One of my favorite teaching experiences was to encounter students from working-class backgrounds whose questions in class or work in assignments suggested a lot of potential. I would give feedback in person or in my comments on course papers, saying that I thought they could go far in academia or in their chosen occupation.

The work conditions that I experienced at WSU could not have been a better environment for me to finally settle down and get to the task of learning how to publish in top-tier sociology journals. This was a difficult journey for me, as I had not received mentoring in this skill in graduate school, nor did I have the chance to take up the challenge in my chaotic years preceding my coming to WSU.

My first challenge was to publish an article from my doctoral dissertation. You may recall that my dissertation addressed how people experiencing pervasive ambiguity collectively construct a definition of the situation to resolve the ambiguity. My first draft of the article was terrible. Mendel's critique of my draft told me that I tended to go on tangents, make poor transitions, use vague long sentences, and did not make a clear and concise unfolding of the theory and the research. In other words, I had a lot to learn, and learn I did—draft after draft. I began the process of becoming my own harshest editor.

The article was finally submitted to *Sociometry*, the top journal at that time for social psychological works from a sociological perspective. It was titled "From Pervasive Ambiguity to A Definition of The Situation." The editor's decision was that I needed to make significant revisions that addressed and countered critiques from the peer reviewers'. This began another learning process. Again, I learned from Mendel how to take on specific criticisms. When reviewers made a good point, you revise, but when the point is not well taken, you counter it with clear arguments. For the rest of my career, I got over my initial anger at harsh reviews after a few days, and then asked myself what I could learn from the reviews, but I did not defer to the reviewers when they were biased or just plain wrong. My first article was published in *Sociometry* in 1973.

While I learned a lot about writing from Mendel, I knew that I had to pursue my interests independently of Mendel's work. I did not want to publish with him not only because our interests were different, but also because I knew that people would assume that any co-authored publication with him was primarily his work, even if I were the first author. This product of sexism meant that I would shy away from any joint publications until I had established my own professional status. I was open to collaborations with others who shared my interests. One of the wonderful resources that the WSU sociology faculty gave me was the opportunity to collaborate with and learn from colleagues. Over the years I collaborated on publications with four WSU colleagues: Jim Short, Melvin DeFleur, Irving Tallman, and Don Dillman. However, I also knew that single-authored works early in one's career were highly valued, so I did not collaborate until I had a few publications in top journals.

My next project was to begin to articulate my objections to the prevailing theories of violence that had been generated by my Violence Commission experience. Jim Short was editor of the top sociology journal, the *American Sociological Review* (ASR) at the time (1972–74). I wanted to publish an article in the ASR challenging the dominant theory of violence, a theory that centered the cause of violence in a machismo subculture. It was important to both Jim and me that there be no favoritism due to our friendship. Jim encouraged me to keep revising my article until he judged that I had met all of the reviewers' criticisms. My article, "Values and Violence: A Test of The Subculture of Violence Thesis," was published in the ASR in 1974. I continued my controversial stance against the prevailing theories of violence by proposing a conflict theory of violence. This article was titled "Normative and Deviant Violence From A Conflict Perspective" and was published in *Social Problems* in 1980. In 1985, I collaborated with Jim Short on a book chapter that addressed the policy implications of this line of inquiry titled "Collective Violence: The Redress of Grievance." The chapter was published in 1985, in the volume *American Violence and Public Policy*, edited by Lynn A. Curtis.

Following on the questions that grabbed me during the Violence Commission days, I turned to challenging the predominant theories of media effects. It's one thing to know that you don't agree with a theory and quite another to come up with an alternative. I worked long and hard to put forth an ecological theory of media effects that involved multiple levels of analysis—macro (e.g., the media system and its information resources), meso (e.g., interpersonal networks), and micro (e.g., individual predispositions). I called the theory A Dependency Model of Media Effects. It challenged psychological theories that primarily focused upon the micro or individual level of analysis, leaving out how the media system's role in society is the beginning of the process of media effects. I note my indebtedness to Richard Emerson, who was one of my professors in graduate school. He had developed Power-Dependency Theory. His basic premise was that control over resources that others are dependent on is the basis of power. The emphasis on media control over information resources that people need to understand the world around them is a basic part of Media Dependency Theory.

While I was developing this theory, I had discussions with Melvin DeFleur, who had his own expertise in the area of media effects. These discussions clarified my thinking, so I included him as second author on an article titled "A Dependency Model of Media Effects," published in *Communication Research* in 1976. This collaboration led Melvin to invite me to revise his well-known book, *Theories of Mass Communication*. I became second author on the third edition, published in 1976, through to the fifth edition published in 1989. The Dependency Model of Media Effects played a large part in these editions. It never became the dominant theory, but it remains one of the major theories of media effects.

During my first few years at WSU, it was not all work and no play. At the center of our circle of friends were Lois and Melvin DeFleur, and Jim Short and his spouse, Kelma. The social life of the WSU community was built around dinner parties in our homes. Fortunately, I loved to cook, although I was not a chef. Kelma Short was much more talented. We had many dinner parties in our home and many more at the Shorts' home. We came to know Wallis and Totsie Beasley and Jack and Betty Nyman, who were frequent guests at the Shorts' parties. Jack was the WSU Graduate School dean. The DeFleurs were always at these events. In very little time, we were part of an interesting group of friends who were insiders in the university community.

The DeFleurs extended our playtime beyond our homes. They were both pilots and had a single-engine plane. We had several adventures as passengers in their plane. We flew to Oregon to see Mount St. Helens after its volcanic eruption caused massive amounts of volcanic ash to cover Pullman and others areas in eastern Washington. When that eruption occurred, I experienced pervasive ambiguity. No one had had prior experience with a volcanic eruption, so it was quite like Tamosu Shibutani's analysis of the dilemma that the Japanese people experienced when the atomic bombs were dropped on them. At first I thought it was a nuclear explosion from the Hanford nuclear facility, about 150 miles away. This ambiguous experience prompted another collaboration on a book chapter addressing the media's role in defining the situation and giving guides on how to adapt. The 1986 chapter, co-authored by Hirschberg (a WSU doctoral student), Dillman (a WSU sociology colleague), and me, was titled "Media System Dependency Theory: Responses to The Eruption of Mount St. Helens."

Another memorable experience occurred when Lois DeFleur and I flew over the Cascade Mountain Range to get our hair done in Seattle. The Cascades are notorious for the danger of icing the wings so that you lose altitude and can't do much to rectify the problem. Well, on one of our trips, we iced up! When I realized the situation, I went into a controlled non-reaction. Nothing was said between us. I had enough experience to know what was happening—we were losing altitude. I was able to keep my cool because I knew that Lois was an excellent pilot with lots of experience and was not one to freak out in an emergency. Lois guided the plane over the lowest pathway through the mountain range. Only when we got over the mountains and the ice started cracking away did we talk about this adrenaline rush experience.

The excitement of travel with the DeFleurs continued with an incredible trip in their single engine plane to La Paz, Mexico, a distance of almost three thousand miles. Our end goal was to go out from La Paz on a hired boat with a crew, to explore the waters of the Sea of Cortez. Not being able to stop to get to a restroom, the men had the advantage of peeing in a coffee can. Lois had some experience with this acrobatic maneuver, but I had to learn that skill. En route, we stopped only to gas up, save for one bad weather event that forced us to land in a little town where the only hotel was quite shabby and had hay-stuffed mattresses.

Once we got to La Paz and boarded our boat, our sleeping arrangements were better when we learned to roll with the sea. The trip was splendid for all of us. We had the beauty of the Sea of Cortez, along with snorkeling, swimming, fishing, and our cocktail hour margaritas.

In 1975, our circle of close friends expanded when Marilyn Ihinger joined the faculty as an up and coming family sociologist. Her soon-to-be husband, Irving Tallman, arrived in 1976 as a visiting faculty member. He was so impressive as a social psychologist and colleague that he was asked to join the faculty as chair of the department in 1977—in the same year that Marilyn and Irv were married. So once again, the faculty was strengthened by the addition of a professional couple. It did not take long for us to become close friends and have frequent dinners at each other's homes. Irv and I collaborated on one of my favorite publications. It was a chapter in a 1979 book edited by Mendel (*Understanding Human Values: Individual and Societal*). Our chapter was titled "Social Movements as Moral Confrontations: With Special Reference to Civil Rights." I think of that chapter as we experience the caustic civil rights struggles of the present era.

My collaboration with Irv came after a major disruption that once again brought Lois's piloting skills into play. Around 1975, an extremely painful bone marrow cancer was discovered in Mendel's spine. It was clear that he needed specialists who were not available in Pullman or at nearby medical facilities. After considerable research, the family decision was made to go to the Palo Alto clinic associated with Stanford University. The challenge was to figure out how to get Mendel to Stanford when he was in extreme pain and could not walk, so he could not take a commercial flight. Lois, bless her, figured out a plan. She arranged for a twin-engine plane that we would hire along with an experienced pilot, and Lois would co-pilot. It was a harrowing flight. We eventually landed at the San Jose airport, where an ambulance had been arranged to take us to Stanford Hospital. Though my relationship with my older sister was turbulent and off and on, I have to credit her with making the arrangements with doctors and the ambulance.

It would take a book to go into all of the turmoil of this period, so I will just summarize the highlights. After a surgical biopsy of the tumor, Mendel went into spinal cord compression that required emergency surgery to remove as much of the tumor as possible. He was left eighty percent paralyzed. All three of his children were on site. Mendel's first wife was very concerned with the welfare of the children, so she came to Palo Alto to support them. Marilyn Ihinger-Tallman pioneered the study of merged families and the challenges they face, and we had to face many of those challenges. The situation required that all of us work together. We were up to that challenge most of the time. I slept, on a cot in his hospital room for the better part of three months with family members relieving me when they could. The generous support of WSU was essential and we were both granted leave.

After the inflammation caused by the surgery decreased, Mendel regained some of his motor and sensory capacities. He was in the kind of pain that could not be relieved by morphine or any other opioid. The medical care was excellent with the exception of attention to what so many people experience in hospitals—extreme constipation. The biggest psychological problem we faced was that Mendel was of the generation that thought of cancer as a death sentence. At the point when I got frustrated enough with his refusal to do physical therapy, I screamed at him so loud that the whole hospital wing could hear me. I said that he was the problem and that if he would only try, he could get better. I think that he got the message that I wanted him to live and he could regain the ability to walk, even if it meant using a cane. Mendel did walk out of the hospital on a cane after many months of our struggle.

In the midst of this struggle, there were other challenges. Early in our stay, I received a call from my internist in Pullman that I had stage 4+ cervical cancer. I had had a pap test shortly before leaving for Stanford Hospital. I had to opt for the less disruptive coning surgery that would only put me out of service for a few days. I was just plain scared. It was a nasty dilemma to have to choose between my health and Mendel's. To this day, I am not sure that I made the right decision as more serious gynecological cancers developed later on.

A more positive challenge was to follow up on the contract to build a home that we had made prior to the discovery of Mendel's cancer. Once Mendel was making good progress, I flew back and forth to check on the how the building was going. I decided that we were going to build an indoor-outdoor pool in addition to the house so that Mendel could continue physical therapy and I could get much needed exercise. It had to have a double-insulated fiberglass housing to deal with Pullman's harsh winters. We had bought the lot below us so that we would have an uninterrupted view of the Palouse countryside. To our shock and dismay, the contractor had built the house backwards, such that we only had a view of a hillside. So, moving into the house was delayed while the contractor made considerable renovations to rectify the situation. Once completed, the single-level home with the pool was a treasure. My career was on hold during this whole period.

There were many other medical events to come, but I will limit my remarks to those that interrupted my career development further and to those that had long-lasting effects upon the Rokeach family and me. In 1977, I was horrified by the discovery that I had multiple gynecological cancers. I had wanted to have children, but that was not to be. The sensitive and skilled surgeon at the University of Washington Women's Center recommended a partial hysterectomy. Losing the ability to have children remains one of the deepest sadnesses of my life.

In the early 80s Mendel's cancer came back such that his spine was basically falling apart. Through a family friend who was an internationally known orthopedist, I located a doctor at the Santa Clara Medical Center. He was about to start an experiment using a surgical procedure for cancer patients that he and others had developed for patients with tuberculosis (TB) that had gone into their spines. The story ended up with Mendel having what I called a sci-fi surgery, using one of his ribs to construct a vertebra along with stabilizing Harrington rods on both sides of his spine. This was the first time such a surgery had been performed on a cancer patient. Mendel spent many months in rehab in Santa Clara. I flew back and forth, trying to keep up both my classes and Mendel's. I had no time to work on publications or conduct research.

Despite the nightmares caused by these events, in 1981 we managed to launch the most important research project up to that point in my career. It involved my first collaboration with Mendel. One of his psychology doctoral students, Joel Grube, was a central collaborator. The three of us pulled off one of the most demanding and exciting projects imaginable. We designed a field experiment that involved three experimental cities and three control cities. The rather ambitious goal was to see if we could use television to change residents' values, attitudes, and behaviors as they pertained to racism, sexism, and environmentalism, and to do so in a natural environment of watching a half-hour television show aired in the experimental cities, but not in the control cities. We had funding from NIMH (the National Institute of Mental Health). Our challenges were many: we had to produce our own television show; create advertising of the program in the *TV Guide* and elsewhere; convince the station managers to air our program in the experimental cities but not in the control cities; construct mail surveys to random samples of experimental and control city residents for both a pretest (before the TV show) and post-test (three months after the TV show); and arrange to have solicitations sent from actual community organizations that focused upon reducing racism and sexism and promoted environmentalism. We deployed both Media System Dependency Theory and Mendel's validated Self Confrontation Theory of Value and Behavior Change. Joel Grube handled the considerable data processing, convinced us to add environmental concerns, and did not get much sleep as he gave his remarkable theory and research talents to the project.

Originally, we had planned to conduct this research in western Washington state, but conversations with Wallis Beasley changed our plan. The western part of the state is much more liberal than eastern Washington. Wallis challenged us to do the research in our own backyard. He was so supportive of the research and influential in our decision to take up his challenge, that we dedicated our 1984 book to him: *The Great American Values Test: Influencing Behavior and Belief Through Television* (Ball-Rokeach, Rokeach and Grube).

We also dedicated the book to the late Ed Asner. We had to find well-known TV personalities that would agree to anchor our TV program. Asner at that time was best known as Lou Grant in his program and in the Mary Tyler Moore show. We contacted his agent, and the long and the short of the process was that Ed agreed to do our program despite the measly amount of money we could offer him. He did so because he thought we wouldn't have a chance of changing people's beliefs and behavior, but we might have a chance of "shutting up the bigots." The co-anchor was Sandy Hill, who at that time was the co-anchor of the ABC morning program. Sandy came on board for much the same reasons as Ed. They both came to Pullman to tape the program, despite Ed's fear of flying and the difficulty of traveling from Los Angeles to remote Pullman. The program was titled *The Great American Values Test*.

Sandra with Ed Asner and Sandra's sister-in-law at the time, Emily Ball, and two nieces, Lisa and Brenda, at the *Great American Values Test*, circa 1980.

Somehow, we met all the challenges with the aid of WSU friends (e.g., Irving Tallman and Marilyn Ihinger-Tallman). The results reported in our book were stunning. Most impressive was that we documented behavior change three months after the TV program aired. This was demonstrated by the responses to the solicitations that came from the real community organizations promoting anti-racism, anti-sexism, and pro-environmentalism. These were mailed to our samples in both the experimental and the control cities. The solicitations asked for support in the form of seeking more information, volunteers, and donations. There was a pre-paid return envelope with the solicitation. We started to notice that there were both positive and negative responses. The negative responses included messages like women belong on their backs or in the kitchen and Blacks should go back to Africa. There were significantly more positive responses from the experimental than the control communities and significantly fewer negative responses. We called the significantly fewer negative responses the Asner hypothesis in accord with his hope of "shutting up the bigots."

Mendel and I had agreed that I would be lead author on the book reporting the theories, methods, and results of our research. Mendel would be second author and Joel would be the third. We had a contract with the Free Press to publish the book. The problem was that I had never written a research monograph (a book focused on a particular project or subject), while Mendel had written four classic works. Fortunately, I had Mendel's experience and instruction. This was our first collaboration, and it was rocky! My learning process entailed harsh criticisms from Mendel—he was not one to sugar coat. At one point, I came down on him for not washing the dishes properly. He came back with "That's not important, but look at this awful sentence"—a classic conflict over sexist divisions of women's and men's work. I don't think my frustrations of yet other rewrites were heard across the Palouse hills, but ultimately, we had our book.

Speaking of sexism, I should comment on a few episodes of sexism in my experiences in the larger university community. There was clearly a problem as shown in a 1971 report done under the university auspices, which found that women constituted only ten percent of the full-time academic faculty. During the time I was a member of the faculty senate, the subject of sexist language came up. I did a fair amount of research to back up my argument that the use of the term, "he" was not inclusive of "her." After I stood up to make my argument, I received any number of comments expressing surprise. These responses amounted to the effect that I was respected—in other words, one of the boys—so why would I take that position in the defense of all women on the faculty.

The other occasion worth mentioning was when I, along with several other women, was asked to explore the possibility of creating a women's studies program. This prospect proved controversial in the larger community and difficult to negotiate with the university and community groups we brought together to set out the contours of such a program. The major objections in the larger university community were the typical assertions that the program was not needed, as the established department curricula included attention to women's history (herstory), sexism, and such. After considerable debate, we did create a women's studies program. Now, it has expanded to become the Program in Women's, Gender, and Sexuality Studies offered as a major or minor in the Department of English.

Not long after we had completed the bulk of The Great American Values Test project, we had another major medical event that took me away from my career for several months. One of Mendel's daughters was diagnosed with CML—chronic myelogenous leukemia. She and her husband were talented lawyers working in the service of workers' rights in the growing fields of Salinas, California. The Rokeach family and the daughter's husband went into full research mode. After many unsuccessful attempts to prevent the leukemia going into blast or the acute form of leukemia (AML), the only option was a bone marrow transplant. This was done at the Fred Hutchinson Cancer Center in Seattle. During this time, Mendel was still very fragile and required frequent tests and procedures.

The merged Rokeach family moved to Seattle for many months. The older sister was the bone marrow donor, and both siblings regularly went through the procedure to give their platelets to boost their sister's blood. One of my most meaningful and inspirational experiences was when Mendel's first wife and I, after a few bumps, came to have more than a functional relationship that continued to deepen over many years until her death a few years ago. To our great sadness, all eleven of the bone marrow cohort died. Mendel's daughter died in 1984, at the age of thirty-three.

My necessary coverage of medical events that were both horrible experiences and disruptive of my career does not communicate the full story of our lives. Mendel and I managed to take advantage of every period of relative calm to enjoy our love life and experience many adventures. We traveled a number of times to eastern Europe, where Mendel had contacts and was well known. These were always adventurous and informative trips. For example, talking with colleagues in Hungary and Czechoslovakia (now the Czech Republic) and observing their lives while still under the USSR challenged my prioritizing of equality over freedom. I saw the everyday effects of living without freedom. As I write, I hear this exquisitely expressed again by the Ukrainians trying to preserve freedom for their country and culture.

On another adventure, I applied for a Fulbright scholarship to the Hebrew University in Jerusalem (1979–80) to challenge the media effects theory of Elihu Katz, one of my idols and a friend. I also applied for fellowships for both of us at the Rockefeller Study Center in Bellagio, Italy. I did this not long after Mendel got out of Stanford Hospital. Mendel was hesitant to go when we were accepted for both, but our joint spirits of wanting to live life won out. We took many other trips, but probably the most improbable was a trip to Japan when Mendel was in a wheelchair. At that time, Japan was totally unprepared for dealing with people in wheelchairs and generally kept people with disabilities out of public view. After arriving at Narita Airport, we ended up having to go under the belly of a building that reminded me of Jean Valjean having to go through the sewers of Paris in *Les Miserables*. The hotel staff was on guard for our every move, including my pushing Mendel up a street to a restaurant where we were met with two men who, without skipping a beat, carried Mendel up the restaurant stairs. Despite these obstacles, we gave our presentations to a conference and managed to have a good time with Japanese colleagues.

Another memorable trip was to Heidelberg, Germany, where we were visiting scholars as guests of colleagues that we had met in Bellagio. Heidelberg was the center of Goebbels's propaganda machine in Hitler's Third Reich. We saw his main theater masterfully equipped with an original sound system. Our many conversations with our hosts validated our belief that the genocide of the Jews, the Roma communities, and many others had been written out of German history at that time (1979). To Germany's credit, that history was later resurrected in the educational curriculum. Today's ongoing attempts in the United States to write out the history of slavery and genocidal destruction of the Native people's culture are a frightening reminder of the power to control what is and what is not taught in our schools.

We traveled from Heidelberg to Munich, on the train, and as we approached Munich, we saw a town sign for Dachau. We asked the hotel concierge if the Dachau concentration camp was nearby. He said he did not know of such a place. We persisted and got tickets to go to the concentration camp. Mendel had immigrated to the United States from a small town in Poland at the age of seven. When he left, the town had five thousand Jews. When he went back to that town many years later, there was one Jew. The sole Jew spent his time uplifting the gravestones of Jews that had been used to create roads by the Nazis. Thus, the visit to Dachau was particularly painful.

I hope I have communicated a more textured picture of our lives while at WSU. I will return now to professional considerations. In 1984, our book *The Great American Values Test: Influencing Behavior and Belief Through Television* was published. The book became quite visible, including in the field of communication. At that time I was the advisor to six

Sandra and Mendel in Poland, 1975.

or seven WSU doctoral students, but their interests did not overlap with mine. They were talented, and I enjoyed working with them, but I did not see the prospect of developing a research team to explore my research interests. This lack of a good match reflected a much larger shift in sociology away from interests in the communication phenomena that had been of prime interest in early eras. It thus makes sense that our book was of more interest to fields where communication phenomena were more central than in sociology.

I made a number of professional association presentations of our research to conferences in and beyond sociology. In the early fall of 1986, I was contacted by Peter Clarke, the dean of The Annenberg School for

Communication at the Los Angeles-based University of Southern California. He proposed that I along with Mendel come as visitors to the school for a mutual look-over, with an eye to permanent appointments on their faculty. The Annenberg School was interdisciplinary with a number of star sociologists on the faculty (Elihu Katz, James Beniger, Everett Rogers, Daniel Dayan). These sociologists were part of the larger movement of sociologists out of their field for the same reasons as mine. I wrote a book chapter about the causes of this movement in a 1986 book edited by Jim Short (*The Social Fabric: Dimensions and Issues*).

The Annenberg School's major focus at that time was on the doctoral program. With considerable financial and other resources, they were able to draw cohorts of exceptional doctoral students with interests that overlapped with mine. As a result of a strong faculty and excellent graduate students, the Annenberg School was highly regarded. We went as visitors to the school in the spring semester of 1986, having been granted leave from WSU. By this time, Mendel's condition had deteriorated to the point where he was in a wheelchair and quite depressed.

My experience during this semester was both wonderful and strange. It was wonderful having fellow travelers among the faculty and the doctoral students, but strange being at a well-endowed private university and school. When I first walked into the Annenberg Building, it was so posh that I felt like I was walking into a corporate building. Mendel's experience was mixed. He was one of the best-known social psychologists in the world. He had his major appointment in the Annenberg School where the faculty and students knew his work. They sought him out with open arms, but his part-time appointment in the Department of Psychology was starkly unwelcoming.

When the semester ended, we returned to Pullman. We had long talks about what we would do if the Annenberg School came through with offers. It was something of a role reversal because I was the main person they wanted. They knew that Mendel was at the end of his career and not in good condition. Mendel handled this well, as his main concern was my welfare. He knew that he did not have long to live. He did not want me to be a single woman in the small town of Pullman where the social life is based on couples. For my part, I was attracted to the advantages of the Annenberg School for my career development. We knew that making the move to Los Angeles would mean losing everyday contact with our circle of dear friends as well as losing our close association with WSU.

We had made a risky transaction during our semester at Annenberg. We bought a single-level, ranch-style, mid-century home conditional on receiving and accepting offers from the Annenberg School. We could not afford the home on our own, but we knew that the Annenberg Trust gave a generous subsidy for the purchase of a home. In midsummer of 1986, we received excellent offers from the Annenberg School, which we accepted after minor negotiations. We moved to Los Angeles into that home in August 1986.

WSU was clearly the launching pad of my career. Mendel and I were deeply grateful for all of the support from our department and from the university. We continued our relationships with our close friends, such as those included in this volume, after our move to Los Angeles. In short, WSU remained close to our hearts.

Chapter 9

From Launching Pad
to Takeoff:
Annenberg School for Communication

The move-in day into our new home did not go smoothly. It was a ninety-five-degree day in August. The former owner had had the HVAC system turned off, so there was no air conditioning. The phone was turned off. This being in the days before cell phones, there was no way to contact the utilities company except for me to spend two hours in a stifling phone booth establishing our accounts. Mendel was in a wheelchair and unable to help with the torrent of boxes. It was on me to try and find bedding so Mendel could lie down, and I could find the other basic necessities. I worked until three in the morning washing clothes and unpacking until I was desperate for a soothing bath. When I went to the bathtub, it was full of ghastly sewage. So, too, were the two showers. Of course, the main sewage line was blocked.

It took a while to get the house in shape at the same time as getting prepared for school to start. One of the problems we had anticipated was that we would often need to drive to school at different times. In his last rehabilitation, Mendel had learned how to drive with hand controls. While still in Pullman, we had purchased a car that we could both drive—me with foot pedals and Mendel with hand controls. It was a Nissan Stanza wagon that did not exactly fit my preference for a powerful car, but it did the job.

We were fortunate to discover that two USC colleagues lived just a few blocks from us. One was a sociologist whom I knew professionally, Malcolm (Mac) Kline, and the other was his spouse and a psychology colleague, whom we had not met previously, Margaret (Margy) Gatz. They reached out to us and became supportive good friends early on. Margy was aware of the unwelcoming treatment of Mendel by her psychology department colleagues and was saddened by it.

Another couple that I had known from professional association meetings was Sara Miller McCune and her spouse, George McCune. They were the founders of Sage Publications. At that time, they lived in Beverly Hills nearby to our Cheviot Hills home. Both of them, and especially Sara, quickly became friends and gave us wonderful support, with many visits and thoughtful gifts. Peter Clarke, the dean of the Annenberg School, and his partner, Susan Evans, gave us generous and frequent support. One quality that all of these friends had was that they were not put off by Mendel being in a wheelchair. I am thankful to all of them for bringing companionship and warmth to the early days of our time in Los Angeles. Margy, Mac, and Sara became lifelong friends.

As so many disabled persons have painfully noted, a wheelchair scares most people. The occupant is treated as a non-person. Fortunately, we had found friends who did not "other" Mendel, but he had trouble accepting himself. This challenge was rectified one day when he parked next to a handsome and vital young man in a wheelchair, and they talked. I'm not sure what that young man said that did the trick. Mendel came home saying that he had finally accepted that he also could be a viable person although in a wheelchair.

There were a considerable number of medical events due to Mendel's decline, but one saving grace was that he had insisted that we get a dog. He had learned to love dogs in our Pullman days. This is quite a feat for a boy from Brooklyn whose only experience with animals as a boy was to have cats to deal with mice infestations. I had grown up with dogs and loved them. The dog we brought with us from Pullman, an Irish setter named Shana Clana, died suddenly. After getting over the trauma of her death, we got a Brittany spaniel named Rachel. Mendel and Rachel were inseparable, keeping each other company when I had to be at the office.

Mendel died in October 1988, at the age of sixty-nine. After his death, Rachel was, as Mendel had hoped, my constant companion and a source of laughter and joy. One positive decision that I made shortly after Mendel's death was to make a donation in his name to fund scholarships for minority students in the WSU sociology department. I was not, however, in good shape. By necessity, I had to overcome my childhood distrust of psychiatry and go into therapy. I was diagnosed as having PTSD—Post Traumatic Stress Disorder. I was granted personal leave from the school for a year.

My therapist suggested that I write the story of my experiences—the nightmare feelings during so, so many struggles that I could not acknowledge until the fight for keeping the "we" of Mendel and me was over. Even in these chapters, I seem to have done what so many women do; that is, play down my trauma and speak more to those of Mendel's. In order to resume my career, I had to spend a lot of time during my year on leave (1989–90) to get beyond the trauma, facing it by writing what I had been through emotionally. I not only had the flashbacks common to PTSD, but I also had the inability to get off what I came to call a high-wire readiness to anticipate and deal with crises. I wrote a long exposition titled *Dying To Live* (December 1989) that I concluded with a poem, "The Circus Left Town." I break form here to include that poem in the hope that it, while not a good poem, nonetheless communicates the emotional challenges I had to resolve in order to return to my professional life.

The Circus Left Town

Stranded on the high wire
Taut force, no net

Yesterday's performance over
Stage of meaning torn down

Suspended in blank space
Unable to stop the act

Balance without purpose
Must stop, muscles ache

Gravity's pull still felt
Fall, balance, climb down?

Wire snaps
Tyranny descends

Performer broken free
Thud of smashing pieces

Perfect freak implodes
The circus has left town

Without the support of my therapist, friends, and family (both Rokeach and Ball), I do not think that I would have emerged from the deep depression and PSTD that led me to write this poem. My best friend, Arline Fujii McCord, has not lived close by since our graduate school days, but she was and is always there for me, either by visiting or on our long phone calls. As odd as it may seem, my most constant support came from Mendel's first wife. She came immediately to Los Angeles when Mendel died. She stayed until the celebration of life ceremony (led by one of the first female rabbis) took place. Many close WSU friends attended. After everyone had gone home, Mendel's first wife called me every day for the better part of a year. She was a talented clinical social worker and that came in handy for me.

Throughout the saga of events before Mendel's death and up to the present moment, the relationships between Mendel's two surviving children and me—my stepchildren—grew to be two of the most important in my life. They are two of the finest people I know. At every turn in my medical and other struggles, they were and are there for me. I also love their children that I have had the opportunity to get to know. I think of them as my grandchildren.

My family was a mixed bag. The only constant was my mother. She would come and stay for weeks to help out. My mother was an amazing person whom I loved dearly. I think whatever spunk I have I got from her. Even though she had her own physical challenges, it never stopped her from seeking to live life. My father would support my mother coming for long periods of time and, sometimes, accompany her for a few days. Of my siblings, I was closest to my younger brother. When he could, he would come and take over all kinds of tasks that needed doing, such as dealing with insurance, fixing things in the house, and replacing broken-down appliances. To my great loss, my brother died in 2005 at the age of sixty-two, leaving his wife of two years. His wife, my sister-in-law, became a lifelong friend who often came to Los Angeles to help out.

My two sisters are a complicated story emanating from our childhoods. There were a number of times when my older sister was an important contributor to medical decisions. My younger sister always had her own problems, so was not really in the picture. The relationship between my sisters and me was dysfunctional in the sense of being a competitive love-hate relationship from the time we were kids. I did develop a close relationship with one of my nephews, his wife, and their son that lasts to this day.

The Rokeach family was so different from my experience of family. It was a challenge for me to learn a new version of family where each member was supportive of the others. Children were at the center and there was nothing that the parents wouldn't do to protect their welfare. I also identified with the progressive Jewish cultural traditions that I had seen tangentially in my undergraduate days, but experienced up close in the Rokeach family. I had become a non-believer in my adolescence, but I adhere to the ethical stances that the progressive parts of the Jewish community hold dear.

I credit my mother, my therapist, the Rokeach family, and close friends for helping me return to the challenge of a productive professional life. Anyone looking at my curriculum vita for the rate of publications over time will see an unusual pattern. The usual pattern is for the productivity of scholars to be high in their early to mid career and then decline as they grow older. In my case, my productivity started to rise at the age of forty-seven, after Mendel died, and continued to increase over the next thirty years until I retired in 2021 at the age of seventy-seven. I think it is fair to say that I filled the void of losing my husband with my work. I did not want to get remarried, as no one could match Mendel or the twenty years of our remarkably rich and deeply loving relationship. I also did not want to marry an older man with the likelihood that I would end up being his caretaker. I did want to take advantage of the considerable resources available to me by way of doctoral students, research resources, and colleagues from whom I could learn.

There is also a pattern of putting my love of theory into doing. By that I mean that I always did theory-guided research, but I increasingly did that in and with the communities I was seeking to understand. One dean of the Annenberg School (Geoffrey Cowan) said to me: "Sandra, your problem is that you are an activist." He meant that in a good way, referring to my desire to contribute to social change with research grounded in the real world. This meant that I began to launch a research project without a preformed theory, but would listen to members of the communities I was studying to learn from them and develop my theory from their superior knowledge of their communities.

Another of my goals was to take advantage of the opportunity to engage and mentor doctoral students who expressed a desire to work with me. I saw the possibility of creating research teams, in addition to working with students one-on-one. I had promised myself that I would be the mentor I wish I had had in graduate school.

The mentoring style that I developed played a central role. Over the years I learned how to conceive of research teams as collegial, not top-down. Each research team member had a voice. Team members' suggestions were discussed and in some important cases adopted. This meant that the doctoral and masters student team members became invested in the project and worked very hard. Socializing outside of the office helped team bonding. The students learned theory and research methods by doing rather than by textbook learning.

After several years working with my teams, I made a decision that proved both fruitful and exhausting. I thought that I was secure enough in my professional status that I did not need to be first author on every, or even many, of our numerous publications. I had seen other research team leaders insist on being the first author, even when doctoral students had played central roles in conceiving of and implementing the project. I thought this undermined their students in a highly competitive market where doctoral students were expected to have several first-authored publications in high-status journals upon their graduation. The exhausting part was that I had to work hard and long with students to teach them how to publish in academic journals.

Team building was not easy. If a student did not play nice with others, I advised that person to seek out another project. I had to think about the various personalities and how each person could be motivated to become a productive team member. I worked with each individual not only on project issues, but also on qualifying exams and dissertation preparation. Over the years the teams varied in size to as many as fifteen students, mostly doctoral. Team building and rebuilding became a major priority as doctoral student cohorts would gain their PhDs and move on to mostly academic positions. My mentoring style became visible to others, and I was awarded several mentorship awards from USC and from my major professional association, the International Communication Association (ICA).

I was not one who particularly liked conventions, but I had to attend them. This was partly because the research projects that I describe below were quite visible in the number of papers we presented each year. I could also introduce my students to colleagues that might offer them jobs in the future. One of the reasons I didn't like conventions was that there were too many men hitting on me, at least before I became too old to be a target. Another was the "how am I doing?" syndrome where many people seemed insecure and needed reassurance that their status in the profession was growing, though, in some cases, that was not really the case.

Of all the research projects we pursued, the Metamorphosis Project stands out as the project that has had the most lasting effect on the field of communication and beyond. Of the many projects we undertook under this umbrella, I focus on two that illustrate my move to doing in-community research where we learned from the communities we were studying. The first addresses the challenges of increasing civic engagement. The second concerns the creation of a local community news site designed to revitalize democracy in one of Los Angeles County's many incorporated cities.

Before I describe these projects, it is important to contextualize the Metamorphosis Project in the larger context of the Annenberg School and Los Angeles. Metamorphosis was born when the Annenberg School was in crisis and the new dean, Geoffrey Cowan, was looking for a keystone project that would enhance the reputation of the school. I proposed a project that would put us into the diverse communities of Los Angeles with the goal of gaining an understanding of how to increase civic engagement. The full project title was Metamorphosis: Transforming the Ties That Bind. The dean accepted my proposal. One of the advantages of a private university is that the dean has a lot of control over financial resource decisions. In this case, there were considerable resources to launch the project with funding from the Annenberg Trust over a four-year period. Subsequently, we received funding from the

First 5 LA Commission, the California Endowment, the National Institutes of Health, and the Department of Housing and Urban Development. The Metamorphosis Project quickly became a graduate student training program in which more than 150 students participated as members of research teams over a twenty-two-year period (1999–2021).

In shaping the project's overarching approach, I learned from my Annenberg colleagues. There was a fortuitous though turbulent merger of faculties, bringing together the Annenberg faculty with the faculties from the Departments of Communication and Journalism in the college in 1992. There were many problems adapting to this new situation. I became co-director of what became the School of Communication, separate from the School of Journalism. As things settled down, there were factions, but not the sort that would cause loss of collegiality, at least not in public. Our school crisis and reorganization challenges came during larger crises in Los Angeles. We had both the uprising caused by the Latasha Harlins killing in 1991 and the Rodney King nightmare in 1992 as well as the Northridge earthquake in 1994.

I benefited from the merger as I got to learn from a rhetoric specialist (the late Walter Fisher) about his narrative theory that emphasized the importance of storytelling. Later in the Metamorphosis Project timeline, I had the good fortune of collaborating with the late Michael Parks, a Pulitzer Prize–winning journalist who came to the Annenberg School as director of the School of Journalism after serving as editor of the *Los Angeles Times*.

The composition of the faculty with regard to gender changed with the merger. When I first came to the Annenberg School, I was the only woman full professor, along with one other woman assistant professor. The administration was all White male, and the only non-White faculty member was a Japanese American. There were no openly gay faculty members. With the merger, the number of women increased to approximately one-third of the faculty. This stands in stark contrast to the population of communication undergraduate and graduate students where women are in the majority. Women in the later years came into the administration, including me. I agreed to be an associate dean of Faculty and Research (2007–9) when a new dean needed someone who knew the university well. I had served on many of the more important university committees. I stayed in that position for two years, only long enough to bring the new dean up to speed. Administration was not where my heart was—I wanted to do the kind of social justice-oriented research represented in the Metamorphosis Project. There are too many Metamorphosis Projects over our twenty-one years of operation to review in this venue, so I will summarize only the two I mentioned earlier.

The Civic Engagement Project

We began with a focus on understanding why some communities have relatively high levels of civic engagement and others do not. We did a literature search and came away not fully satisfied. We conferred with some of the major contributors to that literature, including Jack McLeod, Lewis Friedland, and Dhavan Shah. Our dissatisfaction was with the theory. It seemed that important elements were identified, such as community organizations and local media. We thought there was something missing; namely a dynamic that tied all of the elements together, so that you could come away with a common sense understanding of the process that led to civic engagement. Most of the literature studies were based on surveys of residents and did not go into the communities themselves. We were in search of a theory that would capture the processes that undermined or enabled civic engagement.

We decided that we needed to start by going into several communities. We began with four: Koreatown (the financial and social services hub for the larger Korean community); South Pasadena (mixture of upper middle-class Protestant White and working-class Latino residents); Boyle Heights (largely working to middle-class Latino); and the Westside (largely upper middle-class White with a heavy Jewish population). Ultimately, we employed the same procedures in eleven Los Angeles communities. We did fieldwork to connect with community organizations and opinion leaders. We also did focus group studies with residents and community organizers to try and better understand these communities.

Our approach was multi-method, including surveys, focus groups, field observation, geospatial mapping, communication asset mapping, interviews, and content analyses of legacy, ethnic and social media. In addition to having strong research teams, we were fortunate to have multicultural team members having the linguistic and cultural sensitivities to enable our introductions to and interactions with community members. This capacity proved vital whether it was in Korean, ethnic

Chinese, Latino, Armenian, or African American communities. Our surveys, focus groups, and interviews were in the preferred language of participants, whether that was English or the dominant language of community members.

We came to learn that it was a commonly made mistake to try to learn about a community from elected officials or the most visible and best-funded service-oriented community organizations. Out of all of our engagements with eleven of the diverse communities of Los Angeles, we found that community organizers affiliated with community-building organizations were the most enlightening. Their strategies of mobilizing the community to engage in collective actions designed to bring about change to benefit the community included connecting with resident networks and trying to gain local media coverage. They did so by interacting in culturally sensitive ways with residents and making interpersonal connections with local media personnel. Of all the change makers, I think these community organizers are the hardest working and most devoted.

This knowledge, combined with Walter Fisher's emphasis on the importance of narrative, formed the origins of what came to be our theory, Communication Infrastructure Theory (CIT). This theory is the product of our civic engagement project, but it also became the theoretical orientation we applied in subsequent projects. CIT has two basic components: the storytelling network and the communication action context in which the storytelling network is set.

The storytelling network has three parts: (1) residents in their interpersonal networks, (2) community-building organizations and (3) local media. Storytelling is the dynamic process that links these parts. The theory can be understood by thinking of two different types of communities. The first community has (a) effective community-building organizations that have community organizers in direct touch with residents talking about a local issue; (b) residents actually talk with one another about a lot of things, but that includes stories about the issue; and (c) there are local media that residents consume and that cover the issue. In this case, the three elements are dynamically connected each to the other through storytelling. This community has a strong and integrated communication infrastructure. That is the ideal storytelling process that enables civic engagement.

The second community is the worst case for civic engagement from a CIT point of view. Residents may talk to each other about their families, dogs, or travails, but they are not talking about community issues. This is largely because they are not connected to community-building organizations or they lack such organizations, and they do not have or consume local media covering the community and its challenges. There is no storytelling apparatus to draw attention to issues or to act on them.

Actual communication infrastructures vary along the continuum of these best and worst cases. Intervention strategies to increase the level of civic engagement should first determine the strengths and weaknesses of the storytelling network, and then look to fill any missing storytelling links. For example, if there are no local media covering the community, then funders should support the formation of community-involved media in a time when local media are in sharp decline. If residents are not talking with each other about community issues, then the creation of local media could stimulate such storytelling.

The communication action context (CAC) includes such features as the quality of the schools, public spaces, goods and services, transportation resources, street safety, and childcare and healthcare resources. It also includes the ethnic makeup of the area, the availability of work in nearby places, and the nature of law enforcement in the area. These CAC features can constrain or enable a strong storytelling network. For example, if residents live in an area with unsafe streets, only fast-food restaurants, no high-quality grocery stores (food deserts), no safe public parks, ethnic conflict, or few work opportunities, they are likely to have to go out of their residential area to meet everyday needs. As a result, they miss the opportunity to interact with residents in what we call "comfort zones" or places where they feel they belong, and where it is easy to get to know their fellow residents. This environment may contain so many everyday life challenges, that residents have little time or motivation to connect with community organizations that are addressing the conditions undermining people's ability to be civically engaged.

In my upper middle-class neighborhood with safe streets and a great public park with a great deal of other advantages, dogs are a major way that I have gotten to know and build relationships with people in my area. Once we get over praising each other's dogs, we may start to talk about the neighborhood. Our present focus is to rant about the so-called gentrification that is destroying the architectural coherence of the area. This leads some of us to connect with community organizations that are trying to deal with this issue, thereby strengthening the link between residents and community organizations. Legacy media (radio, TV, and newspapers) as well as new media (e.g., Nextdoor, podcasts) periodically covered this issue. As a result, there are storytelling connections between residents, community organizations, and local media in my area. So, you can see that the Civic Engagement Project's development of Communication Infrastructure Theory not only provides an overarching theoretical orientation to subsequent Metamorphosis Projects, but also affects how I see my own neighborhood.

Before I turn to the second illustrative Metamorphosis Project, The Alhambra Project, let me give you an idea of what I did other than work during this twenty-one-year period. One of my favorite activities was walking with my dog to our wonderful park and letting her run. Rachel, the Brittany spaniel, died at the age of fifteen. A few years later, my good friend and colleague Margy Gatz, found a way to convince me to get a new dog. Her neighbor had just gotten a standard poodle puppy, and the two of them insisted that I meet Charlie. I had always thought of poodles as frou-frou French dogs that rich people got to show off. They gave me books to read that convinced me I was wrong. Poodles were German water hunting dogs with that ball at the end of their tail up in the air to signal where the poor bird was. So I went to see the remainder of the litter and fell for this small standard poodle puppy. My mother named her Jenny, so Jenny it was. Jenny was as smart and easily trained as Rachel was not. More important, she was everything I could have wanted and needed—a loving companion.

I also found relaxation in taking care of my yard. I am still in the mid-century home that Mendel and I moved into in 1986. It has a spectacular view of the San Gabriel and San Bernardino Mountains and a lot of Los Angeles. After Mendel died, I refurbished the home without losing its classic mid-century inside-outside architecture. I hired people to help me redo the small but wonderfully private backyard. Then I would mellow out by weeding and pruning to my heart's content.

I did try a few romantic relationships. The sex was fairly good, but the relationships were going nowhere. Most of the men that I found sexually attractive were either married or gay. I came to think that it was unfair that so many of the beautiful and sensitive men were gay. Some of them became close friends.

I kept up my love for travel. I am not one for cruises. I love the excitement of learning something about cultures new to me. I have had the good fortune of not having to go on group tours. With one or another friend, I traveled to Kenya, India, Ireland (Northern and the Irish Republic), Vietnam, Cambodia, Indonesia, Israel, Cuba, Wales, France, Germany, Hungary, Spain, Japan and my family's countries of origin, England and Scotland. It was usually possible to arrange personalized tours to go well beyond the usual tourist sites. On some of these trips I got to enjoy my love of driving, having to adapt to a manual transmission and figuring out on which side of the road and car to drive.

Yosemite is my favorite domestic site. I took many trips there with the advantage of being able to stay at my good friend's (Sara Miller McCune) lodge at the south end of Yosemite Park. If I had the good fortune of choosing where to die, it would be in the majestic beauty of Yosemite. With all of

Sandra with her beloved poodle puppy Jenny.

these foreign and domestic travels, I found that I had a pretty good natural eye for photography. I had hoped to take photography classes in my retirement, but circumstances have not allowed that up to this point.

Unfortunately, during this time I had to deal with a number of medical crises. I had two different breast cancers, rotator cuff surgeries, a broken shoulder, a fractured vertebra, and sepsis. On top of these events, my mother had a nasty stroke that left her unable to speak and demented. I could not leave her in a skilled nursing facility where I saw patients being treated like sacks of potatoes. From 2004 to 2019, Mother lived with me until she died at the age of 103. My practice of always having a team leader on each Metamorphosis Project paid off as the research went on when I was out of commission.

Having given you an idea about what I did other than work, I conclude this highly selective review of Metamorphosis Projects with a twelve-year (2008–20) intervention designed to strengthen a storytelling network in the city of Alhambra. I retired from USC in 2019, but the Alhambra Project continued until late November 2020. In this project I go from diagnosing to putting CIT theory into practice.

Sandra with her mother in 2006.

The Alhambra Project

The Alhambra Project was a collaboration that came about when the late Michael Parks (a close friend and journalism colleague) approached me with the challenge of working together to use the CIT approach to launch a local media nonprofit with the goal of increasing the level of civic engagement. Throughout his distinguished career until his recent death in January of 2022, Michael saw local media as an anchor institution for creating and maintaining a democracy. At the time of our intervention, there were no local media in Alhambra, save for a Chamber of Commerce monthly newsletter published in English when many residents were monolingual in Mandarin.

The city of Alhambra, located in the San Gabriel Valley area of Los Angeles County, is diverse. At the time of the 2010 census, the major ethnic groups were ethnic Chinese (53 percent, largely first and second generation); Latino (33 percent, largely third and fourth generation); and White (14 percent, the old timers who used to constitute the majority). Alhambra was chosen as our intervention site because prior Metamorphosis research had shown it to have an extremely low level of civic engagement and was a manageable sized city of approximately 87,000 residents with its own city governance and school district.

In 2010, city council elections were canceled because no one ran against the incumbents—a validation of our prior research with regard to a low level of civic engagement. There were a few community organizations, but these were not focused on community building, and they did not have community organizers on staff. City council meetings were almost devoid of participation by residents. Taken together, this community came close to our worst-case scenario in terms of its relative absence of a storytelling network. Residents had no local media to speak of and no community-building organizations, leaving residents without the means to know what their local government and other institutions were doing that may affect their everyday lives.

We didn't launch our Alhambra Source community news site until 2010 because we had a lot to do to learn from community residents and to conduct research of the same kind we had done in other areas. We conducted surveys, focus groups, city officials interviews, and were often in the community making field observations (e.g., location of communication hotspots where residents gather and talk with one another). One of the most important things we needed to learn was what residents wanted to know about happenings in their community. We learned that their top concerns were the schools, traffic congestion, pedestrian safety, grocery stores and restaurants that served their ethnic preferences, gentrification, and pollution of the environment. We also learned that most residents could access an online community news site and many residents were using social media.

Our interviews with city office holders were memorable. The mayor, the rest of the city council and the city manager all told us in no uncertain terms that we were neither needed, nor wanted. They said that a local media site would just rile up a quiet and happy city. In their view, all residents had to do was to look at "their" accomplishments. As in many of the eighty-eight cities in Los Angeles County without local media, there was an old boy network (in this case, with two women) with members circulating from one city office to another. The superintendent of schools was also wary of our developing the site.

The unexpected exception was the chief of police. When he found out that one of our early community volunteers was expert in the social media form most often used by ethnic Chinese residents at that time (Weibo,

The Alhambra Source key personnel.

now replaced by WeChat), he reached out to us to ask if he could develop a Weibo system for the police department. One of their major problems was communicating with the largely monolingual Mandarin-speaking Chinese first-generation immigrants. Our volunteer did create the system for the Alhambra Police, and this system was subsequently adopted by other police departments in and beyond California.

We committed from the get-go to having the community involved in the creation of our site and its operation. We began by putting together an advisory board. Pre-launch of our site in 2010, the board included community-engaged journalists and people we came to know who had either grown up in Alhambra or who were current residents and were committed to being a part of creating a local media site to enable civic engagement.

Once we launched the Alhambra Source in 2010, community engagement expanded. Our first editor (Daniela Gerson) masterfully put together groups of community contributors whom she and other dedicated professional journalists trained in how to write their own stories for publication on the site. Community contributor groups were a diverse representation of the community and varied in size from ten to twenty members.

Anywhere from seven to eleven doctoral students were directly involved, along with our project manager, Evelyn Moreno, who was bilingual in English and Spanish. Nancy Chen (bilingual in English and Mandarin), along with Evelyn, coordinated team efforts. Michael and I were the overall project leaders. All stories had to meet the standards of professional journalism. Our goal was to give transparency to policymakers' decisions that residents told us they wanted to know about along with everyday events that community contributors told us were of interest to residents. Once the site was launched (2010), residents could also access us through every kind of social media that emerged over time.

The Advisory Board expanded once our site was up and running for several years. A major reason for this expansion was an exciting development of community building organizations. These were composed of residents who were tired of the lack of transparency and an intransigent political infrastructure that did not involve residents in their decision-making. They saw the Alhambra Source as giving voice to unheard dissatisfactions with policymakers' decisions with regard to the schools, historical preservation, the parks, pedestrian safety, and environmental hazards, among other issues.

The most impressive example was the formation of Grassroots Alhambra in 2014, a community-building organization with community organizers. This organization spearheaded by Eric Sunada and his colleagues grew to over five hundred members. Its primary concerns were environmental justice and gentrification. With a link to a responsible local media venue and its talented membership, the organization had many successes in altering or stopping city council plans. For example, they stopped an agreement that had been made by the city with developers who planned a major development on a Superfund (environmental waste) site. Our advisory board grew to include those who spearheaded the creation of these community organizations, thereby increasing the diversity of the board and increasing our links with community organizations.

We had many struggles as time went on. We had the enmity of the political power structure. There were open attacks on us in the chamber of commerce newsletter. One memorable attack came when, in his monthly column, a mayor equated us to the kind of cyberbullies that made teens commit suicide (go figure!). We faced constant struggles to gain the funding to survive. While we did develop a membership base, this was not the kind of community with the cultural practice or the resources to donate sufficient funds for our operation. We did get a generous contribution from Sage Publications and the Annenberg Trust and small grants from other sources. We joined national organizations offering fundraising workshops. These were designed more for news sites that served upper middle-class White audiences, not for our working-class diverse community with many first- and second-generation immigrants.

Without going into all the workshops and community events we held over the years, I will focus on one collaborative event that laid the seeds for major change in Alhambra's political infrastructure. Prior to the 2018 midterm elections for city council, the Alhambra Source joined in a coalition of the Alhambra Teachers Association, Grassroots Alhambra, the Alhambra Preservation Group, and the Alhambra Latino Association to hold a "Kids and Candidates Forum." The forum was designed for the community to hear the seven city council candidates respond to questions posed by high school youth. Approximately 420 people attended. Only three candidates accepted our invitation. They were all women—an ethnic Chinese, a Latina, and an Anglo. No incumbent participated. Of the three who did participate, two were elected to the city council and the third subsequently became a member of the all-important planning commission. Of the many sustainable changes resulting from this election, probably the most important were (a) a greater voice for grassroots citizens' concerns; (b) the appointment of new and more progressive minds to the city council and city commissions; and (c) a significant increase in citizen attendance at city council meetings.

Michael and I came to view our community news site as a catalyst for change by enabling the development of an Alhambra storytelling network to achieve our goal of increasing the level of civic engagement. We had to close down the Alhambra Source in November 2020 due to lack of funding. While Alhambra lost its local news venue, the link between residents and community organizations that was spawned during our twelve years of operation remains. It broke our hearts to go dark, but we remained gratified that our journey led to sustainable change.

Looking back at the twenty-one Metamorphosis Project years and my larger professional and personal life, I am thankful for the many ways in which friends, colleagues, and universities supported the evolution of my career and the joy I had in its pursuit. Even though I was a sociologist outsider, international and national communication colleagues rewarded me with election to offices in our major association, the International Communication Association. I was elected to the board of directors, chair of the Mass Communication Division, and chair of the ICA Fellows. I am also recipient of their highest mentorship award, and served on many other association committees.

The Metamorphosis Project ended as a graduate student-training program upon my retirement from USC in 2019. It did not die as a research enterprise, however. Many former students (now colleagues and friends) carry on the tradition in their own endeavors. There are CIT-oriented projects now addressing any number of social issues. These include many projects in US cities and towns, but also in many countries around the world, such as Korea, Japan, England, Hong Kong, Greece, and Singapore. This cornucopia of Metamorphosis Projects is the ongoing legacy of our work.

All of my mentoring and team-building efforts have paid off in numerous other ways that have given me lasting happiness into my retirement years. The zeitgeist of team members supporting and teaching each other has lasted well past their graduations. The Metas, as they call themselves, are a friendship network that continues to operate as a support group, helping each other

Sandra receiving recognition as an ICA Fellow at the ICA annual
conference in Montreal, 2008. Also pictured are Sonia Livingstone
and Peter Monge.

with their professional and personal lives. They also continue to help me.
Given my medical condition and COVID-19, I have had to live pretty much
in isolation. I could not have an eightieth birthday party. On that day, Evelyn
(my project manager for eleven years) showed up with flowers, balloons, and
a treasure that was the best present I could have received—a scrapbook with
pictures and tributes from thirty-two Metas. I sat down with the scrapbook
and my first Scotch in many moons, laughing and crying with joyful tears.

As I reflect on the larger worlds I traversed over eight decades, I am
both encouraged and discouraged about the status of sexism, racism, clas-
sism, discrimination against non-heterosexuals, and all the other "devia-
tions" from the norm that intersect to form a mosaic of who we are and
how we are treated. I am encouraged by the success of historical and
ongoing movements to push doors open to women, non-Whites, and
LGBTQ+ peoples—at least in academia and other professional circles. I
am discouraged, even fearful, by the omnipresent dangers to that progress. Historical and now gross economic inequality along with the decline
of unions have kept the equality door shut to the vast majority outside
professional circles. Civic storytelling networks undergirding democracy
have fallen, leaving a vacuum into which fascism thrives. From my perspective, hope lies in local communities with community organizers and
local media addressing shared concerns, thus affording a bridge across
troubled waters.

As I look back on my career, one regret I have is that I could not be a part of a larger movement of women in sociology who took up the challenge of taking on the American Sociological Association's strong resistance to acknowledgment of sexism within the organization. Pamela Ann Roby recounts the origins of this movement in her 2009 paper presented at the annual meeting of the American Sociological Association in San Francisco: "The Women's 1969 Sociology Caucus, Sociologists for Women in Society and the American Sociological Association: A Forty Year Retrospective of Women on the Move." In 1969 I was at the University of Alberta in Edmonton, Canada, commuting back and forth to Washington, DC, for my Violence Commission work, far away from the locus of these pathbreaking groups of women sociologists.

I conclude my personal story with the satisfaction I feel in having taken up the challenge of growing, challenging, and doing in both my professional and personal life. I feel privileged to have had a life of being able to be myself. This is partly because of my irreverent nature and refusal to either conform to traditional female roles or to unquestionably accept dominant ways of thinking. I prize autonomy, but the living of it would not have been possible without the support of family, students, friends, teachers, and the universities that I have included in my story from childhood to the present.

Epilogue

Glancing Back, Eyeing the Present, Looking Toward the Future

When I look back and ask when I knew I wanted to be an academic, it was in my junior year of undergraduate studies. By that time, I had examined the alternatives and knew that I wanted to have a career that maximized autonomy. I did not want a career that entailed a nine-to-five job or that prohibited sufficient attention to family life. I did want a career that allowed me to follow my curiosities about the social world around me. It would have been helpful to have had a female mentor to inform me about the struggles I would face as I enumerated previously. All my undergraduate mentors were male and likely ignorant of those struggles, including those who encouraged me to go to graduate school in sociology.

Despite the obstacles I did face, I would do it all over again. In addition to the rewards of mentoring graduate students, as noted in my last chapter, I was able to mentor, even sponsor, younger female colleagues in the way I wish I had been mentored and sponsored. I think the primary attributes that I had and that are required even today when the barriers to women in academe have lowered, are a capacity for hard and sustained work, a willingness to challenge whether it be administrative policies (e.g., childcare) or established theories, and high self-esteem.

The immediate context of departments, schools, and universities in which I worked had important consequences for my ability to attain my professional and personal goals. I never experienced the stereotypical nasty context that some of my colleagues at other institutions faced, save for conflicts over mine and other colleagues' Vietnam War protests at Michigan State University. There were two wonderfully conducive contexts, but for different reasons. The first is Washington State University, a land grant public university set in its rural Palouse countryside. The professional and personal support I received from the higher administration on down to my sociology department was what I needed to be able to undertake hard and sustained work, challenge established theories, and feel that I deserved to have high self-esteem.

There were not the bevy of resources for research that I encountered at the second context—the private University of Southern California and the Annenberg School for Communication. I was shocked when I first entered the Annenberg School's building which looked more like a corporate setting with a tiled lobby, not the linoleum floors of WSU. It was a little off-putting. I came to learn that this private institution set in the diverse city of Los Angeles had both the resources and the city context that I needed to do the work I wanted to undertake at that point in my career. My advice to my young women colleagues has been to look beyond salary and status to the context in which they will work as an academic: Is it collegial and is it in the right geographic setting?

Of course, academe has undergone swift and profound changes since my time. With the COVID-19 pandemic and the rise of authoritarianism, academe in general, and the social sciences in particular, are under much more stress. I empathize with both my academic sisters and brothers experiencing the stresses that come from so many directions. These include declining enrollments, contestation of fact-based knowledge, and objections to substantive inquiry into the many isms—race, gender, sexual orientation, et al. In the face of these developments, supportive networks and networking seem especially important.

I am by nature an introvert. While I had close collegial networks, such as the WSU sisters present in this volume, I was not a talented networker in the larger profession. As I noted previously, I went to conferences out of a sense of duty to my advisees. My hope is that the women academics of today can take advantage of the now well-formed local and national networks of women and supportive men to buttress their capacity to pursue their careers while relishing the challenge of defying the odds.

Marilyn Ihinger-Tallman

Chapter 10

The Anomaly:
A Working-Class Background

My path towards becoming a sociologist begins with very few childhood experiences that indicated my life would move in that direction. Rather, events as an adult, including becoming a single parent with five children to support and obtaining three degrees, led to my subsequent career at Washington State University, culminating in two four-year terms as department chair.

I'd like to begin this chapter asking you to conjure an image. You've no doubt at some time or another noticed a large flock of birds swooping and swishing across the sky—flying one direction then suddenly, the whole mass changing direction, flying right, or left, up or down. Schools of fish do the same thing under water. And I believe humans do this as well—at a much slower pace, mind you.[1]

For the first thirty years of my life, I was flying smack in the middle of the flock, behaving very normatively, traditionally, and for the most part, happily. However, at age thirty, my life turned upside down and I found myself leaving the flock, heading in quite another direction. This was in 1967.

Although I didn't know it at the time, this happened close to the beginning of the second wave of American feminism in the United States. Many give credit to Betty Friedan's book, *The Feminine Mystique*, published in 1963, that set the stage for a major change in women's perceptions of their roles and place in society. The social "flock" changed direction, and society opened up new opportunities for women that were rarely thought of when I was growing up.[2]

That is not to say that every woman was in lockstep with the prevailing norms of the time. After WWII there were many women who stayed in the workforce, and many who moved forward in higher education. As did my two esteemed co-authors of this book.

Contrary to my two colleagues, my life from birth to the time I was sixteen was very stable. I lived in the same house I was born into until I was married at age eighteen. And to be honest, there were few indications (e.g., goals, dreams, wishes, or otherwise) that I would end up becoming a professor of sociology.

I was born in Colton, a small blue-collar town in Southern California in the middle of the Great Depression (1936) to a family that now numbered six. The national birth rate that year hit an all-time low of 2.1 births per one thousand women. The average family size in 1940 was 3.67, so my family was above the norm in that sense. In 1936 my father, Frank, numbered among the 25 percent unemployed and, at age forty, was considered "over the hill," and too old to hire. Out of work, with few prospects, he left the family in California to go back to Minnesota to his family's farm to work for his younger brother who farmed and who owned an Allis-Chalmers agricultural equipment dealership. He worked on the farm or in the store and sent whatever money he earned home to my mother.

My parent's marriage was very strange, hard for me even today to figure out their dynamics. My father was prejudiced and authoritarian, and I believe he deeply loved my mother, Ola. She, on the other hand, was miserable, I later figured out. She was thirteen years his junior, married just one month after she turned nineteen, to a man her mother picked out for her.

While I was growing up my father was the parent I followed around, watching him build things, handing him tools. But mostly I was reading, playing with paper dolls, or playing alone. In retrospect my mother was not a notable figure in my life when I was a child. During the war years she earned money doing childcare for one or two babies or toddlers while their mothers worked at the nearby Air Force base. They occupied most of her attention.

During most of my childhood my father was an angry man, expressing his inability to provide for his family by yelling and scolding—mostly while at the dinner table. He never was a violent or abusive man, but the shouting, mostly at my oldest sister Beverly (Bevi), was enough for me to develop into a person who didn't want to be noticed. In the early 1940s he was hired by the Pacific Fruit Express, a company associated with the Southern Pacific Railway. This company made refrigerator cars that shipped California citrus fruit across the nation by rail. His labor entailed using a jackhammer and he did this until the late 1940s. At that time, he developed a hernia from the constant hammering and spent some time in the hospital. When he was healed, he went back to work as an electrician's assistant. When that person retired my father took over the job as head electrician. He held this job until he retired.[3]

As I remember his stories, his wages were very low. In 1939 the minimum hourly wage for workers covered by the Fair Minimum Wage Rates (Fair Labor Standards Act, 1938–2009) was 30 cents an hour.[4] I think he

Marilyn's parents Frank and Ola Pachke in the late 1940s.

earned less than that. My father worked six days a week, and on weekends and evenings he worked on and about our house—building an upstairs addition with two large storage closets, two bedrooms and a bath, turning the garage into a rental house, building a large, covered patio in the back yard, with a brick barbecue grill, and, for us girls, constructing an elaborate playhouse that had electric lights, a doorbell, and screens in the windows. Although church attendance was an important activity while he was growing up on the farm in Minnesota, until I was sixteen my father never went to church with us. He said Sunday was his only day off and didn't need a church to be religious. On the other hand, my mother was the superintendent of the nursery school and her church attendance with her children was routine every Sunday. My brother and I earned a badge every year for perfect attendance. I only stopped my church attendance when I married.

As I mentioned, my mother was never a dominant person in my life. She was just "there." I was closer to Bevi, who was eight years my senior. She has been my female role model for all my life. When I was small, she would take me with her when she worked on Saturdays cleaning the beauty shop where my mother had her hair done every week. I remember the two of us scooting around the linoleum floor on rags, polishing the floor that she had just waxed, and singing. When she went to college (while living at home) I would cue her on the roles she played in the university theater department. I remember learning about Elizabeth Barrett Browning because of one of the plays she was in. To me, she was an "intellectual," someone I wanted to emulate. She was no doubt the one who put the expectation of college attendance in my mind. She encouraged my reading habits, and I spent a lot of time in the city library and loved my time there. After Bevi graduated from the University of Redlands in 1948, she married Karl, a fellow student who also was very influential on my development. He became a renowned artist, and he and my sister opened a whole new world of art for me. Once, when I was twelve, the two of them took me into Los Angeles to an art show and then out to dinner at a restaurant where the tables had white tablecloths, linen napkins, and crystal water glasses. We also attended a movie that was a filmed opera (which I found rather boring). That day made a lasting impression; going to operas and eating out were luxuries my parents could not ever afford.

Marilyn and her mother Ola Pachke in 1972.

Marilyn's sister Beverly (Bevi) visiting her in 1972. She raised
Marilyn and encouraged her to go to college.

In terms of books, my second sister Janis (six years older than me) was the most involved. I still have two of the books she gave me for a Christmas gift when I was eleven (*Penrod Jasper* and *Daddy Long Legs*). While I was in high school, she was working in a San Francisco library and sent me a list of the top twenty-five books "everyone should read," encouraging me to read them all. One of the most vivid memories I have of her is when she was in community college (I was twelve): she would frequently send me to the small grocery store around the corner to buy her a pack of cigarettes. She always said I could have a nickel to spend on myself.

My brother Raymond was two years older than myself. He was mostly a pain in the tush while I was small, pounding me when he could. When I was in seventh grade and he was a freshman in high school, however, he suddenly decided I was "okay"—I had girlfriends—and we became friends. When I got to high school, we would double-date sometimes. A couple of times my mom sewed a skirt for me and a shirt for him out of the same material and we would wear them on the same day. No one noticed.

One thing that stands out about my mother is that she loved to read (probably as an escape) and visited the town library frequently, bringing home stacks of books—mostly detective or mystery stories. She must have been the one that introduced me to the library, getting me a library card, and taking me with her on some of her many visits. I remember as a middle-schooler wandering among the "adult" section, looking at all the book titles, and later, when I was older, checking out books of plays to read. Interestingly, I can't recall that there were many books in our home, except for a few Bible-story books. My father did receive a weekly labor newspaper, which I read with interest, as did my oldest sister, but I doubt that my father did. A staunch Republican, he was anti-union. My mother, on the other hand, quietly voted Democrat, always canceling out his vote at the voting booth. Interestingly, as adults Bevi and I both reside in the liberal camp while Jan and Ray are conservative (on the moderate side) Republicans. I think it was the influence of that newspaper more than anything my parents ever projected that gave me progressive views. We never talked politics in my childhood home, except for the frequent ranting of my father against the Roosevelts. I think this emphasis on books, reading, and learning are the closest ties to my eventual career.

There was one experience in my early schooling that impacted my life and values. I remember few of my teachers' names, but my sixth-grade teacher, Mrs. Mahary, was particularly memorable. After an assignment to write a short story, she read aloud "the very best story in the class" which, to my great surprise, was mine. When she handed it back, she told me that she wouldn't be surprised if someday I would grow up to become a writer. That made me proud, and it widened my world view just a little.

I enjoyed high school; I was competitive enough to get good grades, and I had good friends. I tried out for cheerleader and didn't make the cut, but was an officer in the Latin Club, on the debate team, and held a senior class office. I dated often enough and went "steady" with two different boys during my four high school years. One of them gave me a love of country music and the other introduced me to jazz, which I didn't "get" at all. When I was a senior, my English teacher also commented favorably on my writing ability. I remember being asked to read aloud in class a short story we had been asked to write. Surprisingly, fifty-five years later a classmate from that class told me at a class reunion that she had never forgotten that story. While I had forgotten the plot, she recited it and it all came back. I had written a murder mystery with a "gotcha" twist at the end.

My childhood world was very narrow. Our town was divided by railroad tracks and the north side was all white and the south side was all "Mexican." I had no interaction with any of the kids in my high school who were from south of town. My grammar school had been all Anglo. In high school in the early 1950s I can't remember that there were ever any racial episodes. One of the girls in my circle of friends had Mexican friends, but I didn't.

Overall, my life was very uneventful until 1952 when I was a junior in high school. I was fifteen, my two sisters had married, and my brother was leaving home to start college at UCLA. That summer my parents and I took the train to Minnesota for our annual trip to visit my father's relatives. The plan was to visit in Minnesota followed by my mom and me going on to Maryland to visit my mother's sister and family. My mother had been ill following an incident with a bus door that slammed shut on her leg, causing her to fall and hit her back on the curb. After that accident she could never keep any food in her stomach, and she became bulimic. Over the years she was hospitalized several times because of loss of weight and malnutrition. Ten days after we arrived in Minnesota, she entered Mayo Clinic's nutritional program in Rochester, Minnesota. At that time, my father left to go back to work in California, and I spent the rest of the summer on my aunt and uncle's farm.

After my mother was discharged from the Mayo Clinic, she and I took the train to Chicago where she put me on a train to go back to California and school and she went on to Baltimore to visit her sister. I arrived home at 5:30 a.m., on my sixteenth birthday, met by my brother, his date, and my boyfriend. We all went out to breakfast before going home.

My mother never really came home to stay after that, until several years after I was married. She did return home from her sister's that Christmas in 1952, but one day in early January when I came home from school, she was gone. Disappeared. My dad had no idea where she was. No note, nothing. She had taken her clothes, her hope chest, and a few things from the kitchen. A few days later we found out from a family friend (who had helped her make her getaway) that she went back to Maryland where her sister lived.

So, it was my father and me for my last two years of high school. With a steady income, and only one rather passive daughter at home, the yelling was gone, and he was easy to get along with. He worked, I went to school, and I spent a lot of time with girl- and boyfriends. He would do the cooking and we both raced to see how fast we could clean up afterwards. I don't remember when the house cleaning and the laundry was done, or who did it.

My mother did return home at least once a year. In retrospect I think it was so that she would not be away from her husband for an entire year, which would put her in the category of abandoning the marriage. My father accepted her leaving and sent her what little money he could. The story of their marriage would take up an entirely different volume. Eventually, my parents did divorce and both remarried. I graduated from high school in 1954, when I was seventeen.

Thinking about this now, I can't say how my upbringing sent me in the direction of becoming a social scientist. I was unaware of social status differences except that due to my father's improvements to our home it was larger and more comfortable than the homes of my friends. I had no exposure to race differences, since I had no exposure to children of other races. Even though my father was bigoted, he worked with Mexican men and to my knowledge never berated them. His biased rants were aimed at politicians (only the Roosevelts) which went over my head except to take note and then ignore them. Bevi and Karl and my civics class in high school were more memorable in shaping my political views.

Notes

1. While the majority of people in any group seem to follow general norms, hold similar values, and act according to general prescribed roles, after an undetermined period of time a major change takes place and people, as a group, start to behave differently. At the same time, while each individual behaves according to his or her own individual needs and desires, as a whole, the social group makes a major change of direction, similar to the birds' turn to the right, the left, up or down—notably, with class, race, gender, political and religious views accounting for differences.

2. This movement was given impetus much earlier during WWII when many women went to work outside the home to replace the men who went to fight. Many experienced some discomfort when, after the war, they were encouraged by the media and politicians to return to homemaking roles. That was the fertile ground in which Friedan's book landed (Betty Friedan, *The Feminine Mystique*, New York: W. W. Norton, 1963.

3. My father attended one year of college in southwestern Illinois after high school, and then was called back to the farm because his older brother left to fight in WW I. My father hated farming and dearly wanted to go to war. But there was a great need to produce food for the armed services and his labor was needed on the farm in Minnesota, not in France. Only one farmer's son could go to war if there was no other alternative for help with growing food. During the war years he completed training in automobile mechanics when the winter workload was light. My dad left Minnesota and the farm as soon as his brother returned from France. He spent three years at Bliss Electrical School in Washington, DC, becoming a certified, licensed electrician. My mother attended high school until the end of her sophomore year at age sixteen (not uncommon in 1924), then went to work in a photographer's studio. In 1926 her mother returned to Massachusetts to get her and took her to California to meet the man she would soon marry.

4. US Department of Labor Wage and Hour Division. History of Federal Minimum Wage Rates Under the Fair Labor Standards Act, 1938–2009. Prices and Wages by Decade 1930–1939. University of Missouri Library Guide.

Chapter 11

From Naiveté to Eyes Wide Open:
Two Degrees Later

I've got to say, my naiveté astounds me. Neither as a child nor as a teenager did I recognize or acknowledge the value that my father or mother put on education, as exemplified by my father's own struggle to get an education. Despite the lack of money in our family, my siblings and I all went on to higher education, including law school and two PhDs. I must have absorbed it through osmosis, for the only wishes I can remember ever holding were to have four children and to be "educated"— in the loosest sense of the word. I wanted knowledge: to learn about philosophy, psychology, history, etc. However, I have no memory of taking the necessary steps to go to college: that is, consider where I might go, when to take the achievement tests, etc. None of my close girlfriends had college aspirations (all four of my best friends were married within a year after high school graduation). My last steady boyfriend attended San Jose State College, but we never talked about college, and I didn't ask how he went about preparing for admission. I was totally clueless.

It was during the summer after high school that I heard that a new campus of the University of California had opened in Riverside, a nearby town. I would never have considered going off to Los Angeles to attend UCLA like my brother had, but having a UC campus right here at home, I could manage. My father drove me over to Riverside, and I filled out the necessary papers, paid my $52 tuition for the first semester, and found out what else they needed, e.g., letters of reference, high school grades, etc. In retrospect I must have had a high school transcript with me to give to them. The campus had opened the previous January 1954 with only 127 students and 65 faculty. In the beginning UCR was intended to be a small liberal arts college. Becoming the "Harvard" of the west was the aspiration. However, in 1959 the regents voted to make it a general campus with graduate instruction, professional schools, and the like. That is what I returned to in 1967.

My first experience in college was to be expected. As clueless as I was, I went to the general orientation in the auditorium without paper, pencil, or information as to what it was all about. I asked a young man sitting next to me—Bob was his name—if he had an extra pencil and piece of paper I could borrow so I could take notes. Seven months later, we were married.

My first semester grades were all over the place: two A's, a B, a C, a D, and an F. Note that I was being courted at the same time! One compliment I remember from my English professor was that a paper I wrote for his class was "better written than—," (a local newspaper reporter), a woman I had never heard of. I considered it a compliment. Second semester I left in good standing with all C's. But by then I was married and was expecting our first child. Needless to say, I did not go back to the university in the fall of 1955. Bob did, however, and he graduated at the end of that academic year.

My first pregnancy was followed by four more in the next six years. During this time my husband taught elementary school, continuing in graduate school to become a school psychologist. He first earned a school psychologist credential, followed by a master's degree, then entered the PhD program. I credit his educational experiences as a guide to follow when it became my own journey to go back to the university.

For the first twelve years of my marriage, I was a wife, mother, and homemaker. In 1961, when I was pregnant with my youngest, a friend suggested that we take a course together at nearby Mt. San Antonio Junior College in Pomona, California. The first class we took was Sociology 101, followed by Sociology 102. After another year and two more semesters—Psychology 101 and 102—my husband moved the family closer to the Claremont graduate school he attended, and he commuted to his school psychology job. I had to stop taking classes with my friend, but I kept going by myself. This time around I was getting all A's. It was liberating to get out of the house once a week, and to be learning the subject matter I had always wanted to know—and excelling in the process. My community college course work ended when my husband accepted a job at George Peabody College in Nashville, Tennessee, in May 1966. He still had his doctoral dissertation to write, but he was hired in an assistant professor tenure-track position that began in the fall. We left California in August 1966 for Nashville.

Marilyn and Bob Ihinger Christmas shopping in 1962.

That move would prove to be a pivotal turning point in my and my children's lives. Without going into great detail, in December 1966, after being in Nashville for four months, Bob declared he had fallen in love with his research assistant and wanted a divorce. No counseling, thank you. He was moving out. Which he did, then came back, then moved out again. After recovering from the shock of it all, I can say I was no longer naive. I figured out how to access our small savings account (it was not in my name) to get the money I needed so that I could get my kids and myself and the furniture back to California. I found us a place to live in Claremont with the help of friends, and I enrolled back into UC Riverside—all from Nashville. I figured if I had to support five children, I needed a college degree. I did manage to take two classes that spring semester at Vanderbilt University, which was located across the street from the Peabody campus. A neighbor who befriended me watched the kids while I went to class. I reciprocated when she also took a course at Vanderbilt on her way to becoming a school librarian. One important life observation I learned at that time is that there are many generous and caring strangers and acquaintances who come out of the woodwork to help when they see someone in trouble. Those last eight months in Nashville were made tolerable by such people.

So, in August of 1967 I moved back to California where the children had friends, schools, and an environment they were familiar with. And, importantly, it was where my sister Bevi and her husband Karl lived. My father wanted me to return to my childhood home, but I evaluated the educational systems in both places and chose Claremont, a college town. I rented a house from a professor and his family who were taking a sabbatical, enrolled the children in their various classes at their old schools, enrolled in classes at UCR, and found a part-time job, thanks to work-study funding. My youngest was just starting kindergarten so I found a half-day caregiver for her and for the others after school until I could get home from Riverside every day, a half-hour commute. My college education began in earnest.

My first year of classes at UCR counted towards my degree, plus the various night courses I had taken amounted to almost another year of college work. Thus, when I started classes in the fall of 1967 I had almost junior standing. I declared a social science major and took classes in both sociology and psychology, plus the few requirements still to fulfill, such as language in which I received my F in in 1955. I did not spend any additional time on campus beyond taking classes. My work-study part-time job was with the Department of Rehabilitation in downtown Riverside. I did make a few very good friends who also were returning students, closer to my age. One, in particular, I owe much gratitude to, since he, with his pickup truck, helped me move four times in the next four years.

The first move after the first year was from the sabbatical house into a large rental home of a good friend, promising I could rent it for as long as I wanted. However, I had to move at the end of that year when she and her husband adopted twin daughters and wanted the house back. The next move was to another sabbatical house. That professor was in Germany, supposedly for three years, but the couple divorced during that year, and his wife wanted her house back. The final Claremont move was to a house just down the street, owned by the neighbor who managed the rent payments of the house we were in. She said I could stay in it for as long as I wanted, which I did until I finished two degrees and moved to Minnesota. I must add that to make each move easier on the children I had them pack their own toys—and of course nothing was left behind to give away. Even though we moved around town four times, I negotiated with the school district so the younger children could remain in their same school while the older boys made the natural move to middle school and high school.

It is important here to mention that three weeks after I returned to California in 1967 my husband—soon to be ex—came back to California too. Evidently the Tennessee mother of a twenty-two-year-old woman thought it unnatural for a professor with a wife and five children to fall in love with her daughter. She convinced the president of the college of the same, and Bob was terminated. (This was far earlier than the recent "me too" movement.) He accepted a school psychologist job in Palm Springs, moved his girlfriend there, and they married soon after our divorce was granted in January 1968. The reason I mention this is that his returning to live reasonably close to the children allowed them to visit him every other weekend. This turned out to be a godsend for me because it gave me time alone, free of the responsibilities of childcare, with no worries about how well the children were being cared for. Bob became a better parent after the divorce. I think he appreciated his children more, since he had no more children with his second wife. He was court ordered to pay child support from the Tennessee judge ($75 per child per month) and he did this until each child turned eighteen. At that point he continued to pay each of them the same amount of money while they were in college. (Permit me to brag a little here: all five children went on to get higher degrees. One law degree, two MBA's, a master's in education, and a PhD in geology.) This experience of managing relationships after a divorce, and the interactions that followed concerning graduations, marriages, and the births of grandchildren also influenced my interest in making the study of the family my subfield.

My first year returning to UCR was consumed with a full-time course load, a twenty-hour part-time job with the city of Riverside, and my home and children to take care of. My senior year, 1968 to 1969, was no different. My part-time work-study job that year was as a research aide with a newly hired professor, Irving Tallman. He had just joined the faculty at UCR, coming from the University of Minnesota with a major grant of several million dollars. This was a collaborative grant with three other University of Minnesota faculty, all working on cross-cultural projects. My job involved typing tables of numbers. But it gave me insights into what research was all about, how data could be analyzed, and the marvelous things it told you about people. That job was my first real exposure to social science and what data can reveal. I was hooked.

As the end of my senior year, I was hoping to enroll in the same education program at Claremont Graduate School that Bob had been a part of several years earlier. Its focus was on teaching "disadvantaged" children. I hadn't considered that things do change with time. I talked to the relevant people at the Claremont graduate school, only to be told their grant had not been renewed that year. I had focused on teaching as a career so that I would have the same working hours and vacation times as my children. What to do? A teaching credential from UCR didn't appeal to me.

It was at that point that Professor Tallman redirected my thinking and asked, "Why not stay in the sociology program at UCR and get a master's degree?" I could teach in a community college and still have similar school schedules as the children. Problem solved. I did lose his support as a mentor and friend when he returned to the University of Minnesota at the end of that year. California and the smog didn't live up to his expectations, and he was disappointed in the department. He appealed to his Minnesota department to take him back, and they did. But encouragement and support came from other faculty in the department during the next two years of my master's program.

I can honestly say that I did not perceive any sexual bias or discrimination or harassment during my graduate (or undergraduate) years at UCR. That may be because I was a returning student and older than most other students, and/or because I was doing this while raising five children. I spent little time on campus aside from my classes and job. I found the faculty, staff, and fellow graduate students to be 100 percent supportive. There were two women, Professors Edna Bonacich and Jane Mercer, on the faculty during this time. I did not take courses from either of them as their areas of expertise were different from mine. Contrary to Sandra's experience, my graduate education was facilitated by the male faculty in my sociology departments. My master's advisor was Professor Ed Butler, and he was not only mentored my research project but was very encouraging of my acceptance of the Minnesota invitation. For the two years of my master's program, 1969 to 1971, we were living in Claremont, and I was commuting back and forth to Riverside.

My interest in family sociology became etched in stone my first year as a master's student. I was taking a family course, and one evening I was sitting at the dining room table doing my homework with the kids all around, doing their thing. It occurred to me, why not do my own little case study? Let's do some observations of sibling interaction! I watched, listened, and took notes for a few weeks. What I discovered was a huge surprise. I observed that the three youngest were their own little group. Always together, playing board games, or imagining and creating stories and plays. My oldest son could be found in front of the television while reading a book. He said he could understand both at the same time. My second son was usually not around. He hung with friends, or was off in his room, I'm sure anywhere but with his siblings. There was a lot of competition between the two oldest boys, but little of it played out in my presence. I tend to think now that it was to be protective of me as much as it was that I was oblivious, because they didn't hold anything back in front of their father. I checked with my daughter, and she confirmed—fighting occurred only when they were at their dad's. According to her, at one point when they started shoving each other, their dad told them to just go at it—and I guess that was the end of their physical fights. Both boys ended up going to and graduating from Carleton College in Minnesota. Somewhere along the line they buried their differences, and when my oldest son was being treated for cancer and had to be driven to Mayo Clinic in Rochester, some one and a half hours from Minneapolis, his brother drove him many times. At his funeral his eulogy was the most memorable and brought on the most tears.

So how did I get to Minnesota for the doctoral program? At 8 o'clock in the morning in the winter of 1971 (my final master's year) I got a conference telephone call from Professors Tallman and Paul Reynolds, who were both at the University of Minnesota. Tallman was inviting me to apply to the graduate program at the University of Minnesota, and if I was admitted, he was offering me a research assistant job on his cross-cultural project that was just getting off the ground. I could get my PhD from one of the best family departments in the country, whose family area was led by esteemed Professor Reuben Hill. And I would have financial support during those years.

At the beginning of my senior year (1968–69) Professor Reynolds accepted a position at UCR. He was working on his dissertation, being ABD from Stanford. That's how Professor Tallman knew about him, and why two years later recruited him to the University of Minnesota. I had taken several social psychology courses from Reynolds so he knew my work and evidently thought I would be a good candidate for Irv's new research project.

I recall exactly the time their call came because the children were all in the car and I was on my way out the door to drive them to school when the phone rang. I answered the telephone, and during most of the call the car horn outside honked constantly, and my son was hollering that they were going to be late for school. I couldn't exactly hang up the phone, but I told them many, many, thanks for thinking of me, but I didn't think I could do that. Irv explained that I would first have to get admitted to the department, and if I was admitted, I would have a job for the rest of my graduate education. I thanked them again, but said no. They said to "think about it," and they would get back to me.

After the kids got dropped off and I was driving to Riverside the idea occurred to me, why not? What was keeping me in Claremont? I had no husband to think about, I had made the move from Tennessee to California by myself, I could do the same in the other direction. The next day I asked for opinions from my graduate school friends, and they all said go! I asked a few of my professors and they all said go! So, in August 1971 we went.

I want to send a shout out to Professor Reynolds again, who not only suggested me as an applicant to the Minnesota program and as a research assistant to Professor Tallman, but he was responsible for finding us the perfect living arrangements in Edina, Minnesota. My one and only request when asked was that I needed to live in a good school district. The summer before I moved, Reynolds found the perfect place for us and put down a deposit to hold it. It was an old farmhouse in Edina that stood on two large lots on the top of a small hill. Edina was a very wealthy township; it had the best school district in the twin cities, and upper-class homes surrounded ours, a golf-course was down the street, and a small shopping strip mall just down the hill. Our old farmhouse was an original, before suburbia build up around it, so it was rather an anomaly. But it was perfect for us: enough bedrooms for each of the children, a yard big enough for our dog to run around in, and for building snow forts during the winter. The house next door was of the same vintage. A single mom and her four children lived there, and we became friends. A tiny older house next to hers was occupied by an old couple and these three were probably the only blue-collar homes in Edina.

One of the hardest things I've ever had to do was to convince five children that a great adventure awaited us in Minnesota, and they should leave their schools and friends and go there. (I'm afraid I did say that when I finished my PhD degree I would get a teaching job in California, and we would move back to Claremont.) Four were easily convinced, but my oldest—by then entering his junior year in high school—was the most disappointed. He was the shyest of the children and had just made good friends in high school and was involved in their theater program. In addition, the move to Minnesota was hardest on him because after he spent one year in East High School in Edina, Minnesota, where we moved, his school split the students because of over-crowding, and he had to go to a new West High School several miles away. He did find some stability the following year when he entered Carleton College and spent four very good years there. I should note that even though Carleton was a private school I was a single parent with five children at home living on a graduate school stipend. Two of my sons who went there won scholarships in addition to financial aid due to my low earnings.

Chapter 12

Goal Fulfilled:
University of Minnesota
PhD Program

Because I had taken several classes from one of (now) their own professors, I entered the doctorate program with a few accumulated credits. The family was to be my specialized area of study, with a related three-course "Area Studies requirement" of the program. This was in lieu of a second language. I chose Scandinavia since my mother's heritage is Swedish. So, along with the usual coursework in sociology I also took Scandinavian history, family, and literature. This last course was a very welcome requirement, since I found out how marvelous it was to earn graduate credits by just reading fiction.

In addition to classes, my role as research assistant (RA) was enlightening, but very time consuming. One of my assigned tasks was to interview married couples in the Minneapolis/St. Paul area for Professor Tallman's cross-cultural project. This meant several nights a week spending one or two hours in the homes of white-collar and blue-collar couples. I would drive home after classwork, make dinner for the kids, get them situated with homework or whatever they were working on, and drive back into the city or suburbs to conduct the interviews. My children were all between the ages of nine and sixteen, and the oldest was able to be responsible for the younger ones. I was very lucky: all my children were well-behaved, non-hyperactive, rule-abiding, responsible children and—to my knowledge—did not get into any trouble. I tried to be home before their bedtime, but it didn't always happen if the interview was a long one. I would find a note on my pillow: "Mom, please wash my gym clothes. I need them in the morning."

I made good friends with other graduate students—all younger than me, but I'm indebted to one in particular. Pat came from UCR to the University of Minnesota at the same time I did, as a PhD candidate in psychology. I didn't know her when we were at UCR, but we met at some function just before we left California, and in Minnesota we became friends. She would be the one to come stay with the kids if I had to go to a conference, and if she had to go out of town, her standard poodle Pandy would come to stay with us.

I was also befriended by a young newly hired professor, Jeylan Mortimer, who came to Minnesota in a temporary position. She was assigned an office next to mine in the basement of the West Bank Library. We became acquaintances and later good friends. The next year she was hired in a permanent tenure-track position and continued on to a very distinguished career in sociology.

Coursework and RA work proceeded in the usual manner. After the first year I took the qualifying exam for the PhD program, passed, and continued on with classwork. My RA job now involved evenings at the small-groups lab when the couples who we had chosen from the previous interviews brought their preteen child into the lab to play a simulation career game. This was long before what can now be done with computers, but at the time (1972) it was an ingenious and creative way to record parent-child interaction and decision-making. I wrote my dissertation using these data, looking at parental transmission of child attainment values. In particular, I examined adolescent educational and occupational aspirations and achievement.

After the third year I stood for the preliminary exams and passed all four. I asked Professor Ira Reiss to be my advisor for my dissertation, since by this time I had begun a relationship with Professor Tallman. He moved from boss, to mentor, to friend, to lover, and then to husband over the course of ten years. We were married for forty-one years before his passing in 2017.

I have been asked many times, from many people, how I managed to go through graduate school and raise five children. My response was always, well, I just did it. You really have to do what you have to do. But the lovely editor of this volume said, "that isn't enough." So, what does a good sociologist do? I interviewed my children about their perceptions of the years I was going to school. I was reminded that I had on the refrigerator a rotating list of dinnertime chores: Across the top were the days of the week and along the vertical axis were the tasks. In the cells were the children's initials, rotating up every day: five kids, five chores. Help with the cooking, set the table, clear the table, wash the dishes, and dry the dishes. That scheme eliminated a lot of arguments. I did all the laundry and ironing and on Saturday we shared the housekeeping chores: dust, vacuum, clean the kitchen, clean the bathroom, and outside—mow the lawn or shovel the snow. This last item had to be added after I got a note from the mailman saying that my mail would no longer be delivered until the snow was shoveled off the fifteen front steps. Trouble was, no one ever used those steps except him. We had a long driveway around the back of the house, and everyone came up the hill that way and came into the house via the back door.

The Ihinger home in Edina, Minnesota, where the family lived while Marilyn was a graduate student working on her PhD.

Overall, my parenting was based on responsibility and sharing, with a strong focus on fairness. You divide the slices of bacon so that everyone gets the same amount. I am a good listener and am patient enough to let another person vent until the anger is dissipated and we can talk about the problem. I learned early on that to get a message across to five children you need to repeat it many times. I knew that shouting got you nowhere and the lower your voice, the more a person had to listen to hear you. I knew enough to trust, and to hold high expectations. These ideas served me well later in my career especially when I became chair of a department with twenty-seven full- and part-time professors, each with a unique personality.

My oldest daughter reported that the most special times were when I was not doing homework and we would all settle on my large king-sized bed, and I would read to them. There was music, and dancing, and fun times, but the norm was for them to fall asleep to the sound of the large old IBM typewriter that my father bought me, typing into the night.

Each summer for the four years we were in Minnesota the children spent two months in Texas with their father. When we were divorcing, I insisted that if he were to take one child, he must take them all. Knowing that if it were any other way, I would never be free of the responsibility of childrearing. As it turned out summers were a chance to refresh and retool, for all of us. And their dad was able to be a dad again since he had no children with his second wife. This experience was no doubt why my research interest focused first on siblings, and second on divorce, remarriage, and stepparenting, especially after Irv and I were married. My first publication in the *Journal of Marriage and Family* was titled "The Referee Role and Norms of Equity: A Contribution toward a Theory of Sibling Conflict."

Chapter 13

Washington State University:
A Sociologist's Career
and Retirement

I am truly a fortunate woman, living at the right time, and in the right places. Going back to school, I was on the cutting edge of the second women's movement, and society was becoming aware of a larger place for women. At age thirty-one I was welcomed into an undergraduate program at the University of California, Riverside. It was also a time when education, especially graduate education, was valued and funded. Once when I was desperate for $500 to pay double rent because of one of my Claremont moves, I went to the financial office to see if I could borrow the money. I was asked to sit and wait a few moments and when the clerk returned, she had a check for $500 for me. It was a grant that I did not have to repay. Granted, it was at the end of the school year and the university obviously had some money that had not yet been distributed, and there I was with my hand out! Over time my donations have paid back that $500 many times over. The point is that I have been extremely fortunate all through my life.

Another example of my good fortune: After I completed my coursework at the University of Minnesota and was settling down to work on my dissertation, a call came from a former Minnesota classmate, Gary Lee, who had taken an assistant professor position at Washington State University. He asked me if I would be interested in a job at WSU. At that point I wasn't exactly looking for a job, but WSU had one of the best family programs in the country at the time. How could I say no? He said I had been recommended by Professor Ruben Hill and that I should send the WSU chair of sociology, Charles Bowerman, some needed information. Several weeks later I got a call from the chair, asking for more information. I sent what they wanted and waited for another telephone call. It came soon, offering me a tenure-track position as assistant professor. (In 1975 Washington State University had a policy of not bringing assistant professor applicants to campus.) I accepted the job, and my colleague Gary Lee set about looking for a home for me and the three children I would be bringing. My oldest was going to be a junior in Carleton College (in Northfield, Minnesota) by this time and the second oldest was just about to start his freshman year there. I give Gary a huge shout-out not only for encouraging me to apply for the job, but also for facilitating my move to Pullman, as he found a beautiful rental for us. It was so much nicer and more modern that the farmhouse we were living in in Edina. He was and is a true friend.

One hitch in the move was that my oldest daughter was about to begin her junior year at Edina High School and wanted to stay and live with my best Minnesota friend, Mary Anderson. Mary was fine with it, but I said no, she was too young to leave home, but that if she still wanted to, she could come back for her senior year. Smart me, I figured she would make new friends and the idea would be long gone. But the friends she made in Pullman were temporary themselves. They were children of faculty who were at WSU on sabbatical or were visiting professors. (She claims that that was purely accidental.) As a senior she did in fact move back to Edina to live with the Andersons and had a wonderful senior year with her friends there.

In 1975, my first year at WSU, the days were filled with course preparation, teaching, faculty meetings, working on my dissertation, and running a household with the three youngest children. At this point Irv Tallman and I were committing to a relationship, and we spent a great deal of time on the telephone. The kids and I went to Minnesota for Thanksgiving, and Irv came to Pullman for Christmas. My dissertation progressed slowly, but it did progress. During Christmas break we talked about whether I should look for a position in Minnesota.

Marilyn Ihinger-Tallman and Irv Tallman, together in Pullman, early 1980s.

During the spring semester of that year, all three of the social work faculty in the department resigned—two women and one man, all with PhDs. They were tired of being treated as second-class citizens in the department and conspired to find jobs and quit at the same time. The majority of undergraduate students in the department at that time were social work majors, so the departure of those three faculty members left a huge hole in our curriculum. The faculty voted to reorganize the social work program. That decision inspired me to go to Charlie Bowerman, the chair, and offer a suggestion: Irv had a master's degree in social work from Michigan State University and he'd had a career as a social worker for over a decade before he started the doctoral program in sociology at Stanford. Why not bring him out to Pullman as a visiting professor and have him reorganize the social work program? Bowerman was enthusiastic and supported this idea. By this time the whole faculty knew Irv and respected his reputation as a social psychologist and political sociologist. Irv was happy to come.

During the following summer while all the kids were in Texas with their dad, I was in Minnesota to work on my dissertation. In the fall Irv took a leave from the University of Minnesota and moved to Pullman.

My daughter moved back to Washington, enrolling in WSU as a psychology major and living in the dorm. From 1976 to 1977 Irv reorganized the social work program, and I finished my dissertation, flying to Minnesota in December to defend it—thus completing the PhD program. At Christmastime, Charlie Bowerman approached Irv and asked him if he, Charlie, retired a year early, would Irv take a permanent position at WSU as chair? Of course, there would have to be a national search. That offer entailed some heavy decision-making: Would Irv want to move permanently to Pullman? Could I get a position in one of the colleges in Minneapolis/St. Paul? Should we marry?

The last question was answered when we drove to California to visit his mother during spring break. Before we left, we asked the two children still at home how they felt about us marrying, or not, and they said, "It doesn't matter." In California, we asked his accountant friend, who said, "With five kids to pay for college? No way!" We asked his lawyer friend, who gave us the same answer, and he also said, "No way!" So we called Irv's best friend Dave who, with his wife Renee, flew to California. We got a marriage license from San Francisco City Hall, and three days later drove up the coast and got married by a justice of the peace in Mendocino, California, outdoors beside the bay, with Dave and Renee as our witnesses. Irv also decided he could live and work in Pullman if he were offered the job. Irv had grown up in San Francisco and definitely was an urban person. Pullman appeals most to small-town folks who love the outdoors, with its rural setting and hiking, hunting, and fishing close by. We vowed to make it possible for him to get an "urban fix" at least every six weeks. And with an academic schedule, national meetings to attend, NIMH meetings quarterly (for four of the years anyway), and season tickets to the opera in Seattle—only a five-hour drive away—we could make it work. And we did. Closer to home, to support his interests, we became enthusiastic supporters of WSU basketball and football. We bought season tickets to both sports and sat with friends in the bleachers of both sports venues and tailgated before many of the home football games. During the last five years of his career at WSU, Irv held the post of Faculty Athletic Representative (FAR), representing the university at the meetings of the National Collegiate Athletic Association (NCAA). This post provided him with the opportunity to get out of town for those meetings several times a year as well.

Marilyn and Irv after their marriage ceremony in Mendocino, 1977.

One of the ancillary benefits that came from our union was that Irv brought his two daughters into the family. I could not wish for more delightful stepchildren. They were in their teens when we married, but they were welcoming and kindly towards me.

We added another child to our family from 1979 to 1980 when we hosted a student from Sweden in the exchange student American Field Service (AFS) program. Agneta (Annie we called her because we just didn't get the right pronunciation of the "g" in her name) became a third daughter. We spent a wonderful year together and have remained close—throughout her college experience in Sweden, her marriage, the birth of her children (we are godparents to her daughter) and now when she and her husband are in the "empty nest" stage. (I should add that we promised as godparents to raise her daughter in Sweden if anything should happen to her and her husband.)

Exchange student Agneta Nilsson, Irv, and Marilyn, 1981.

At WSU I taught a number of courses besides the family offerings. In particular, I was happy to be assigned to teach the Development of Sociological Theory class, a requirement for the major. Introducing the "masters" of sociology to undergraduates was fun for me. Durkheim's, Weber's Marx's, and particularly Simmel's writings were/are full of insights and wisdom, and they made good observations of the society of their times such that I felt that students had much to gain from reading, at least excerpts, from their works. (I did preface the readings with the caveat that these men were men "of their times" and were chauvinistic and no doubt racist). My students must have gained some benefit from this class since I consistently got high evaluations. I believe teaching this course was the reason I was selected by the undergraduate majors to be the "Most Difficult Instructor" in the department.

Home for Christmas in Pullman, 1982. From top: Robert, Erika, Shannon, Phillip, Lance.

A very fortunate event happened that cemented my chosen topic of study. In 1977 the Department of Family and Child Studies hired Professor Kay Pasley. In 1979 she came knocking on Irv's door, asking him as chair if there was anyone in the department who was interested in studying remarriage? Hmmm. He recommended that she talk to me and that began a twenty-year collaboration that I still treasure. Kay and I worked together on our joint research and writing on the topics of divorce, remarriage, stepfamilies, and stepparenting. In addition to our joint publications, we organized a small informal group of about eight other fellow professionals across the country also studying divorce, remarriage and stepfamilies and we met every year at the annual meeting of the National Council on Family Relations. That social group was as much fun as it was academic. Kay moved on in 1983 to a stellar career at several universities. I stayed in Pullman until I retired in 1999. But we continued our collaboration from a distance, publishing many articles and a few books.

My career at WSU proceeded apace, moving through the ranks in almost the usual manner. My research agenda moved slowly at first and when I came up for tenure and promotion to Associate Professor, I was granted tenure, but my promotion was held back until the next year. This was embarrassing to me, but as Irv said, tenure is what counts. He quoted Ruben Hill who told him to "keep your rank low and your salary high." My teaching evaluations were always excellent, however. So much so that in 1992 I was awarded a Faculty of the Year Award from the College of Arts and Sciences. I also received a plaque given by the Undergraduate Sociology Club in 1994 naming me "The Most Difficult Instructor." It was a point of pride for me.

One of the most important and lovely aspects of my job at WSU was having Lois DeFleur and Sandra Ball-Rokeach as colleagues. Sandra and Milton, her husband, lived around the corner, and the four of us became good friends. They showed us how to fish in Lake Mary Ronan in Montana, although Milt got a little disgusted when Irv caught his fishing line in the boat's outboard motor, and Milt had to tow us back to the dock. (I did mention that Irv was an urban person). It didn't help either when I heard the fish that Irv had reeled in and was taking off the hook let out a cry. I refused to try to catch any more. Instead, I read aloud a novel I was reading about Marin County, California,[1] that was so funny we laughed aloud, and Milt yelled across the water that we were scaring the fish. But he didn't

Milton Rokeach, Marilyn, and Irv fishing in Lake Mary Ronan, 1980s.

hold that against us, and we shared many years of conversations, travels, and good times. I attended my first seder at their home. Milt was seriously ill during many of those years, and Pullman seriously lacked a sophisticated health system. He and Sandra spent a good deal of time in a Seattle hospital and in the Stanford University hospital in California. In 1986 Sandra was hired by the University of Southern California as a professor in the Annenberg School for Communication and Journalism and Milt was appointed a one quarter position in the psychology department and a three-quarters appointment in sociology. Their leaving was a huge loss to both for us as well as for the department.

One important characteristic of Sandra's that was missed in the department when she left was her ability to cut through an endless discussion during faculty meetings, summarizing differing points of view and calling for a vote. She knew exactly the point at which to do that.

I also owe a great debt to Milt for helping me become a better writer. Once when I was feeling down because I had just had an article rejected, Milt told me to come over and he would go over the paper with me. We sat in the sunny bay window of his living room and for two hours went over my paper, word by word, sentence by sentence, him showing me a better, more effective way to write the article. To this day I can't recall the tips he gave me, but they are engrained in my brain and have vastly improved my ability to write.

When they moved, we lost daily interaction with Sandra and Milt, but we still had Lois. From the beginning she was my mentor. She took me to get a make-over in Macy's in Moscow, Idaho (no spas in those days), introduced me to aerobics and the gym, and cautioned me, as did Sandra, to establish an independent career different and apart from Irv's. She became a regular at our dinner table after aerobics when we would come home to a dinner prepared by Irv. I missed her presence in the department when, after returning from a sabbatical year at the University of Chicago, she became dean of the College of Arts and Sciences (formerly the College of Humanities and Social Science) at WSU. We continued our social lives together until she left Washington State University to become provost at the University of Missouri in 1987.

Being an academic gave me the opportunity to travel to places that otherwise I would never have gone. I presented papers in Jerusalem; Lisbon, Portugal; and Uppsala, Sweden. In 1981 I traveled to China with twelve other women sociologists who were teaching in universities around the country. Our group participants were all members of Sociologists for Women in Society (SWS), and we were sponsored by the All-China Women's Federation. In 1981 China was still very much under the influence of Mao Zedong's ideology, and there were thousands of bicycles on the streets of Beijing and very few cars. Brown or blue trousers, blouses and caps were worn by everyone. My photos of Beijing, Hangzhou, Yangchow, and Shanghai depict a China long gone. My photos show entire areas of Beijing that were torn down over the next four decades, making way for skyscrapers and modern apartment buildings. I owe a huge debt to Irv for not only his constant support but for his stepping in and teaching my classes while I was in China. He had taught family classes in Minnesota, so he was comfortable taking over for two weeks of the three (one week spring break) while I was in China.

In 1985 the university established a Washington Higher Education Telecommunication System (WHETS). This added distance learning to the curriculum (live interactive classes), which was an innovative way to reach students on our newly formed branch campus in Vancouver, Washington. I taught three times to distance learning students, using an overhead to show outlines, charts, etc. to the students in Vancouver, Washington, and visiting the distant campus at least twice during the semester. This was a prelude to 1989 when the university officially opened branch campuses in the Tri-Cities (Kennewick, Pasco, Richland), Spokane, and Vancouver, Washington. Two of our Pullman campus colleagues moved to the west side of the state to teach sociology classes in Vancouver.

In the early 1990s the campus officials decided to make a universal requirement of all incoming freshmen students to take a World Civilization class. This required course was divided into two parts, one offered each semester: time frames being pre-history to 1500 and 1500 to the present. Faculty across the campus and in different departments were recruited, and in preparation there were workshops every summer for several years as well as ongoing meetings throughout the semesters for which the faculty were paid a stipend. Being chair at the time, I signed up for this wanting to be sure sociology was included. There was a span of five years lead time to prepare for this daunting task and I admit I gained an extraordinary amount of respect for my fellow colleagues who were in the various departments across campus. I learned a lot from them during this preparation time. The historians were best suited for the task, but since the faculty were allowed to teach either of the two courses (you picked which time frame you wanted to teach) in their own way, given certain parameters (e.g., the specific geographic areas/cultures we were to teach were mandated) they each taught it according to their area of expertise. For example, the music faculty emphasized the music of each era and area; the English faculty focused on literature. As a sociologist I emphasized social institutions (family, religion, the political system, etc.) in each society. Confessing that it was the most intensive learning experience of my career would not be a misstatement. I taught the course twice—1996 spring semester before taking a sabbatical and spring of 1998 after I returned. The first two years the course was offered to students who volunteered to enroll. Once the general freshman population was required to take the course it was harder to teach. Fortunately, my two courses were filled with students who volunteered to take it. It was not an easy course to teach or take, so no doubt there was some pushback and eventually it was discontinued.

In 1987 the department was due to choose another chair. I was approached by several faculty members to put my name forward, and to tell the truth, I was ready for a change. The position of department chair sounded good to me. In spring semester 1988 the faculty voted me in, and I was chair for two four-year terms, from 1988 to 1996. One of the things I tried to do as chair was to create a better sense of community. Among other things, I instigated at the beginning of every fall semester a departmental BBQ/picnic for all faculty, graduate students, and incoming graduate students. We reserved one of the local parks for a day at the end of August for a potluck picnic. Professors Charles Tittle, Irv Tallman, and sometimes Louis Gray would do the BBQ grilling and there was always a game of softball or frisbee, with several small children adding to the mix. I do think it served the purpose I had intended. Happily, the tradition has continued to this day.

When I took over the chair's position in 1988 there were, I think, twenty-seven full and part-time faculty and about sixty masters and PhD graduate students. The number of undergraduate sociology majors had shrunk because the criminal justice program was moved out of the department. We had four women on the faculty at that time.[2] Fortunately, Professor Lisa McIntyre was one of those women. She was a master teacher, and thanks to her efforts at teaching Soc 101, Introduction to Sociology, I credit her for greatly increasing the number of our majors. Her 101 class size was regularly over 500 students, taught in a large lecture hall. Even there, her humorous, engaging, and dynamic teaching style drew many students to our discipline as majors.

Irv Tallman manages the grill at one of the departmental picnics, c. 1990.

One of the first things I did when I became chair was to meet individually with each of the faculty. I took each of them to lunch or to coffee and discussed with them their perceptions of the department and their place in it; what were they working on, and what did they need to accomplish that; where did they see the department heading? I got a lot of feedback, and I heard a lot of bitching, but overall, I got a good idea of the entire faculty's ongoing research, and state of mind regarding the department and the discipline. In my mind, my primary job was to facilitate the faculty's research and teaching efforts and to present the department to the dean in the best possible light. In order to create a better sense of community, I instigated the fall semester BBQ that I mentioned earlier. We already had in place a day-long faculty "retreat" at the beginning of fall semester, which was in truth, a day-long faculty meeting (with lunch). One thing that I consider a very important social salve is to be generous with the phrase "Thank you." I was appreciative of any (and most) suggestions the faculty gave me, and those from graduate students as well.

Every year I made the effort to send a handwritten thank you to the graduates of our department who contributed money during our annual departmental fundraiser. The sociology department was way ahead of not only the university as a whole, but of many universities in soliciting developmental funds from their graduates. This was accomplished thanks to the innovative telephone methods of one of our faculty, Professor Don Dillman. Dillman was the Director of SESRC (Social and Economics Sciences Research Center) on campus, formerly the Public Opinion Lab. In the early days he recruited undergraduate and graduate students to make telephone calls to our alums asking for donations using the lab facilities.[3] Over time the university development office took over this fundraising function but for many years sociology was the only department benefiting from this idea.

Thanksgiving week, and the ones preceding and following the holiday, I wrote a short note to those former graduates who donated money to the department. Whether the contribution was $10 or $100, they all got the same thank you. Several hundred of these were mailed each year. We did have computers, and the capacity to mass mail, but my thinking was if they took the time to write out a check, I would take the time to thank them. Only problem, they wrote one check, and I spent many an evening writing multiple thank you notes! I don't know if the labor was appreciated, but I felt good doing it.

During my tenure as chair, I introduced several innovations that I was particularly proud of. We established three new funded awards: The Short Award, in honor of Professor Jim Short, an esteemed and senior faculty member; a teaching award in honor of Professor Joe Martini, a favorite teacher and faculty member who oversaw our graduate teacher training program who had recently passed away; and the Ann Madison DePew Memorial Award, established through the generosity of DePew's family in honor of one of our early sociology graduates. I started a departmental library, consisting of monographs and some of the classic sociology authors (Weber, Durkheim, Simmel, etc.) for graduate student use. Donations for the library came from the faculty, often those retiring and wanting their books to have a good home. We instituted a one-year subscription to the *American Sociological Review* for our first-year graduate students, and for those students further along in the program the department provided a small amount of money for the purpose of conducting original dissertation research. Finally, we put into the graduate curriculum a semester devoted to developing teaching skills before graduate students were placed in the classroom as instructors. Professor McIntyre taught this seminar and shared her classroom expertise.

My good fortune was taking over the administration of a well-funded, respected department. In our earlier years (1940s) the department was headed by men who went on to positions in upper administration in the university, especially Wallis Beasley and Tolbert H. Kennedy. Beasley was chair of sociology and went on to become academic vice president and later interim president. Kennedy was dean and recruited Beasley, whom he met in graduate school. Both men were from the south and had experiences with traditional Black colleges. They opened the doors of the department to aspiring Black students who now number among the most respected in the discipline: William Julius Wilson, James Blackwell, Charles U. Smith, Franklin Wilson, Edgar Epps, and many others. Our department gained a national reputation for producing outstanding sociologists of color. In 2004 the department received the DuBois-Johnson-Frazier (DJF) Award given to persons or institutions for work in assisting the development of scholarly efforts in the DJF tradition. Many of our Black PhD graduates numbered among the presidents of several sociological associations, including ASA. However, beginning in the late 1960s when diversity was beginning to be appreciated or mandated, other doors in more prestigious institutions opened for students of color and it became harder to recruit African American graduate students to Pullman.

One of the important topics currently being addressed in universities around the country is the harassment of people by others in positions of power. As an adult, many of my friends and acquaintances are/were former faculty-student couples, as was I. Propinquity is a powerful concept, and people who work closely together are often drawn to each other. As an undergraduate student I personally was never hit on or harassed by either faculty or fellow students. My friend Carl was always only a great friend, and I was seldom on campus except for classes. As a graduate student at Minnesota, I did hear gossip about at least one faculty member's affair and was advised never to enter the elevator if Professor X was on it. In Minnesota I dated two unmarried faculty members, one of whom became very important to me, but for the most part I was involved with Irv. As chair I had two major incidents dealing with harassment. Both involved faculty members as harassers, one male and one female. Both cases were resolved, one by upper administration and one by me. After leaving WSU both faculty members moved on to distinguished careers in the discipline.

My years as chair were gratifying—except for the last semester of the last year. During that year several events occurred that wore me to a nub by the end of my term. One involved a faculty member whom the faculty voted to deny tenure, and three others involved graduate students. There was a graduate student with a gun who went around for days waving it and threatening one of our faculty members. Another clearly mentally unstable young woman kept making heavy breathing midnight telephone calls to me, to the associate chair, and one other faculty member, until I had the police trace the call and she was sent off to be helped, we hoped; and yet another involved two of our graduate students who tried to explain chaos theory to me all the while creating chaos in the department and the university. The faculty eventually denied them admittance to the PhD program, and they left after two years.[4]

In 1991 one of the department's graduate students spent four months in jail because he refused to reveal information regarding an animal rights break-in on campus. This graduate student was out of town at the time but had agreed to let some animal rights activist friends stay at his home.

While they were staying there, they did some damage to offices in the vet school. When he refused to reveal his conversations with his friends after he returned, he was jailed. He cited the 1989 ASA Code of Ethics in his refusal to answer questions that pertained to his dissertation research, which centered on radical social movements. The faculty rallied behind him as did the American Sociological Association which issued a Brief of Amicus Curiae on his behalf. The case was resolved when the student answered questions associated with the break-in but none that would reveal any confidential conversations or information.

I want to add that during the troubled times, as well as when things were going smoothly, John Pierce, dean of the college, always had my back. For years sociology held a special place in the university insofar as the sociology faculty valued writing and research and brought grant monies to the university. Our publication rate overall was very high, and the faculty brought in millions of dollars in grant monies to the university.[5] The social psychology program was ranked near the top of all academic departments in the United States during these years, as was the family area. Our sociology faculty were the first to recognize the coming ecological crisis, beginning with the publication of Professor William Catton's *Overshoot*.[6] Catton, along with Riley Dunlap and Gene Rosa are credited as leaders in establishing the area of environmental sociology within the discipline. I should add that Dean Pierce was always very supportive of our efforts, and even if he couldn't give me everything I came asking for, he did listen and gave good reason why he couldn't grant my request.

When my second term as chair ended Irv and I took a year's sabbatical from 1997 to 1998, and then stayed at the university for another year to pay back our leave. We retired in January 1999. Sometime during my last term as chair, Dean Pierce approached me about an opening in his office and asked if I would like to become associate dean. I thought about it a long time but said no, thanks. I looked at the job description and knew that with that job came obligations to attend evening events, as well as maintain a year-round academic calendar. I thought of what Irv had given up coming to Pullman. He had retired from the sociology department a year before but was still working half-time as WSU's Faculty Athletic Representative to the NCAA and was thinking of the good times we would soon have in retirement in the San Francisco Bay area where he grew up.

By the time my eighth year as chair ended in June 1996, I was ready to sit in the sunshine and do nothing. A very extraordinary gift the faculty gave me when I retired were two trees planted in my honor in front of the Alumni Center on campus, along with a brass plaque with my name on it as chair of sociology, 1988 to 1996. They truly were my friends as well as my colleagues. (I have sent several of my children to visit those trees in the ensuing years!) I honestly think that being the mother of five taught me many skills that came in handy when I chaired the department, including: listen, repeat yourself, be patient, and keep your ego out of it.

After I retired, I set upon writing a family text that Kay and I had contracted with Roxbury Press. It was the perfect time for me but unfortunately, Kay was still in the midst of a very busy career at the University of South Carolina at Greensboro and didn't have the time. I contacted a colleague I had met while on sabbatical who was interested in collaboration, so Professor Teresa Cooney and I wrote the book I always wanted to teach from. It was a broad, all-encompassing examination of the family: as a small group and as an institution, using systems theory as an orienting principle. We were aiming for an audience of students in several disciplines: social work, child and family studies, and sociology. The textbook was published in 2005: *Families in Context*. Our approach was very creative and innovative in our minds, but apparently it was not exactly what a family faculty member, or any of the disciplines we sought, needed as a textbook. It never became a bestseller. But I was satisfied and consider that I left academia with a flourish!

I began these chapters with an analogy about bird behavior and my life. As I consider the timing of the three careers reported in this volume, I realize that all three of us were outliers. The others, probably more than me. Lois and Sandra chose a direct path toward an independent career going directly from college to graduate school to faculty position. They started graduate school in the late 1950s and early 1960s. These were the years when women were barely beginning to make their voices heard. Sandra and Lois were among the first to turn from traditional roles. Their backgrounds induced greater aspirations and more independent behavior than I ever experienced. My path was the anomaly because it was more normative than the others—first spending thirteen years as a homemaker and mother before approaching an academic path (except for those years taking night school courses). Even so, for me it was more with a push than a pull that I returned to full-time college coursework. I have no idea how my life would have unfolded had not that push happened. But I do know that as a result, I was able to have a successful and rewarding academic career. And for that I thank the support and friendship from many, many people.

Notes

1. Cyra McFadden, *The Serial: A Year in the Life of Marin County*. New York: Knopf, 1977.

2. Compare this total to the 2022 faculty: eleven women and seven men.

3. Professor Don Dillman went on to develop a mail and telephone survey technique that has been used nationally and internationally (Dillman: *Mail and Telephone Surveys: The Total Design Method*, New York: John Wiley, 1978). This volume was subsequently updated and coauthors were added; the current fourth edition is Dillman, Smith, and Christian, *Internet, Phone, Mail and Mixed-Mode Surveys: The Tailored Design Method*, Hoboken, NJ: Wiley, 2014).

4. From my current perspective I see that they, being people of color, were reacting against their perception of racism in the university. Their disruptive behavior certainly stirred the waters, but I can't say I saw much change. They did help to sensitize me to the fact that at the time there was no barber in Pullman who could cut the hair of African Americans and students had to drive to Spokane, Washington, for that service. In addition, there was a very limited selection of cosmetics in the student store for women. I did point this out to the store's buyers, and they enlarged their selection. I could do nothing about the barber.

5. For example, Milton Rokeach and Sandra Ball-Rokeach were awarded almost $500,000 for their American Values study; over the years he was at WSU, Riley Dunlap was awarded approximately $500,000. Irv Tallman, Peter Burke, and Vic Gecas were awarded an NSF grant of more than $2 million to study newly married couples.

6. William R. Catton Jr., *Overshoot: The Ecological Basis of Revolutionary Change* (Champaign: University of Illinois Press, 1980). William R. Catton Jr., "Environmental Sociology: A New Paradigm," *The American Sociologist* (1978): 41–49.

Epilogue

Glancing Back, Eyeing the Present, Looking Toward the Future

When I set out on my academic path, I was fortunate to have vicariously "been there before." Having observed the process of my (first) husband's academic journey, I knew the ropes, so called. There were a few bumps in the road, e.g., being sidetracked from a career in elementary teaching due to a lack of funding for the program I wanted to enter, but the substitution and outcome in the academy were so much better.

My entry into academia was at odds with most others who became professors. I truly was a child of my times, marrying early and adding five more people to the boomer generation. To be honest, I would not change a thing. I was able to be home with my children when they were all preschoolers (I was not in the least bored) and when the last child started kindergarten, to pick up my studies again.

Once I obtained an academic appointment and came to Washington State, I was faced with finishing my dissertation (I came ABD), preparing for and teaching courses, participating in departmental activities (i.e., committees), parenting the three children who came with me, and running a household. Whatever expectations I had were submerged. However, while I was getting my master's degree at the University of California, Riverside, I taught a family course at the University of Redlands, and while at the University of Minnesota I co-taught with a fellow graduate student a summer course in the department. Therefore, I knew what to expect in terms of teaching. The WSU department chair was kind, and I did not have much committee work the first year while I finished my dissertation.

Having had a vicarious "preview" of the academic process, I can honestly say that there were few surprises along my own path to obtaining a PhD. I would say that my expectations were exceeded when experiencing how supportive and kind people—faculty and fellow graduate students—were to me, all along the way. I guess I was geared to expect more hostility to an "older" student in their mix. Later, I was informed that when the University of Minnesota faculty were discussing my application, my age (thirty-four) did come up as something to be considered. I was not totally prepared for the high expectations for conducting research and publishing. Although I had an article accepted for publication before I got the WSU job, and I had certainly observed the process of tenure denial due to a lack of publications at the University of Minnesota, it took a while to understand the pressure of "publish or perish." My first husband's graduate degree was in the field of education, and since he had not completed his dissertation at the time of our divorce, I did not know all the expectations, and could not extrapolate, to a degree in the social sciences.

I really did not know what to expect when I assumed the chair position. Mostly I wanted to get to know my colleagues better and find out what resources they needed to accomplish their research goals, assuming they were doing their best at teaching. I took it as my responsibility to do the best I could to provide those resources and to present the department and faculty in the best possible light to upper administration. I found I had a collection of individual personalities, egos, and aspiring scholars that had come together as a community in Pullman. And if we could all pull together to reach mutual goals, we would have an outstanding department.

Based on my experience in the academy—and on the path to getting there—if asked, I would suggest three things for aspiring graduate students: (a) know your stuff: i.e., be serious about your training and don't be lazy; (b) be confident, and know that you can do it if that is what you want (confidence can be real or faked); and (c) be prepared to make lifelong friends. To succeed in this endeavor, my advice would be to work hard, make friends, and expand your social contacts to "network" within and outside of your discipline. Try to have at least one publication before you start the job search these days. The current social scene is not the one that I flourished in. The social and political climate that prevails currently may not be conducive to opportunities in academia. But hang in there. If you want it, you can get it.

Conclusion

Making a Difference:
Cracking that Glass Ceiling

Betty Houchin Winfield

If there are underlying themes in the Troika's stories, they are that they "made do," regardless of the circumstances, they also took risks, and worked very hard. And, by making do, they joined those few other females in their field to put more cracks in that proverbial glass ceiling in the last several decades of the twentieth century and into the first decades of the twenty-first century.

In the process, each of these three women became renowned scholars within multiple sociology subfields: urban drug use and gender, societal violence to media sociology, and family sociology. They each were leaders, and in separate ways, too; as a university dean, provost, and a president; as a major international scholar and director of a massive research project; and as the first female WSU Department of Sociology chair. Their stories inspire those early in academia, those who may feel alone as they too take risks in their research and dare to be leaders.

The Troika began their fifty-plus years in academia as sociologists for several reasons. Some had mentors who suggested graduate work in the field to them as undergraduates. For one, Lois B. DeFleur, her mentors saw her leadership capabilities in the higher education field—from which she fled after one semester to return to sociology. Another Troika, Sandra Ball-Rokeach's experience as an immigrant gave her the natural sociological position as an insider/outsider observer. Her decision was based upon her perceiving the field as young and providing an opportunity for her to have influence. And, another sociologist, Marilyn Ihinger-Tallman, identified sociology as making sense of her own life and family experiences.

All three of these trained sociologists recount their numerous challenges and how they took risks, and, despite often being the only female present, how they persevered. Some of the challenges were tough family situations. Two of them, DeFleur and Ihinger-Tallman, survived philandering husbands, which led to divorces. Another, Sandra Ball-Rokeach, talks about how her husband's debilitating illnesses slowed down her career ascent. Then, another, Marilyn Ihinger-Tallman, had to balance her life as a single parent and keep five children happy while at the same time succeeding during a demanding full-time scholarly career.

All three women felt alone as women and experienced discrimination and sexism. They also faced gender-related academic trials from the beginning of their academic careers. Lois DeFleur had to convince the University of Indiana sociology chair that she should be admitted and would be a resolute graduate student. As a graduate student at the University of Washington, Sandra Ball-Rokeach had to argue that she deserved a fellowship as much as the male graduate students. She also told of a grudging male mentorship early in her graduate school days. All her professors (less one at the last minute), would decline to help her find an academic position; a situation unlike that of her male graduate school colleagues. For the third, Marilyn Ihinger-Tallman had to somehow support five children and become a successful undergraduate and then graduate student.

For all three, there were also the challenges of being one of the very few female academics in a university. As single, attractive women, or whether as graduate students or professors, they faced sexual overtures to the point that for many years one of this group admitted that she did not look forward to national conferences.

At the same time, male mentors saw their potential and encouraged and helped. So, too, did husbands, whether as sounding boards or writing coaches. Even one mother, Sandra's, was a constant supporter. Their validation came in the form of major research articles, highly competitive grants, invited lectures, and campus-wide lectures and teaching awards. They built national recognition as scholars.

In each case, there had to be some give to have a whole life while making an academic career work. As they say, their families impacted their decisions. Two Troika members (Lois and Marilyn) changed universities after their master's degrees to pursue doctoral studies. Marilyn fretted about her children's adjustment when she moved. She also worried that her soon-to-be husband would not be happy moving to the isolated, small town of Pullman after living in a large city at the state university. Sandra recounts the difficulties of providing the intense caring for a husband with serious medical conditions while maintaining a full-time academic career.

For stress relievers these women recount their enjoyment of travel, concerts, and festivals. Physical exertion helped. For Lois it was early morning running, after-work kickboxing, weekend flying, and adventurous physical challenges. For Marilyn it was racquetball and aerobics. Marilyn mentions that child-raising was a great distraction and diversion. Sandra's dogs and yard work helped her relax.

The sociologists "made do" with their circumstances, yet they took risks and grabbed opportunities. Lois DeFleur took the highly unusual step of doing research in Argentina before her doctoral work even began at the University of Illinois. During her first professorship, Sandra Ball Rokeach moved to Washington, DC, as a research leader on the President's Commission on the Causes and Prevention of Violence. Often mistaken for a secretary, she was the only woman in a fifty-person professional staff. Marilyn Ihinger-Tallman risked it all when she moved her entire family from warm southern California to Minneapolis for her doctoral work, and then moved again to Pullman, Washington, for her first full-time academic position.

These three women also recounted the opportunities they dared to undertake. Lois, not only as a pilot, but also as the first female Air Force Academy distinguished visiting professor. Over and over, she became a "first," in administrative positions at three universities. Sandra took risks by challenging prevailing theories of violence, media effects, and civic engagement and coming up with her own theories and developing research for validation. Marilyn attempted and succeeded in her family-scholarly balancing act, no matter where she lived. She added to the original early family research on siblings, divorce, remarriage, and step-parenting.

At WSU, all three flourished. They found support and fertile ground for their academic endeavors. They tell of quickly going through the professional ranks from being an assistant professor, to gaining tenure and promotion, and becoming among the very few female WSU full professors. They taught hundreds of students, mentored both under-graduates and graduate students, and did major research. Lois's lectures became part of her undergraduate sociology textbook, adopted by major American and international universities. Sandra's major research on American values involved both undergraduate and graduate sociology students as assistants. Marilyn evaluated her research ideas about family in her classrooms while she continued her own investigations.

Each of the Troika established a recognizable research niche and par-layed that work to become a renowned leader. Lois's national presentations on urban youth drug research made her a desirable candidate for a position at Washington State University; and her textbook authorship caused her to be offered the Air Force Academy visiting position and do subsequent research on gender receptivity at a military academy. Her campus leadership as one of few WSU full professor women led her to become the first female dean of the campus's largest college. Four years later, her national presentations led her to become the first female provost at the flagship campus of the University of Missouri. Four years later she became the first female president of the State University of New York at Binghamton. She served there for twenty years.

Sandra Ball-Rokeach was a scientific leader, a scholar/researcher. She spent fourteen years going through the WSU professorial ranks. Her early research and appointment as co-director of the media and violence task force of the President's Commission on Violence led her to become nationally known as a scholar. She spent the next thirty-four years as a professor at the Annenberg School for Communication at the University of Southern California, where she developed an international reputation as she further developed media dependency theory. Now, she is best known for her later work developing communication infrastructure theory and leading the twenty-one-year Metamorphosis project that trained more than 150 graduate students in ecological and multi-method research on civic engagement.

Marilyn's early assessment of the missing gap in sociology family research led to her subsequent academic articles and books that led to her national scholarly reputation about various aspects of families. Marilyn's work was relevant to all three Troikas who ended up getting married, dealing with siblings, or facing the challenge of divorce, remarriage, step-parenting, and merged families.

During her twenty-four years at WSU, Marilyn Ihinger-Tallman became the social, emotional, and administrative leader in the Department of Sociology. She was elected for eight years as the first female chair of the Department of Sociology with mostly male faculty of twenty-seven. She quietly managed the extant faculty divisions and greatly enhanced the sociology department's programs.

For all three Troikas' careers, their research impacted their sociology subfields and made real world differences. Lois DeFleur's early research of urban teens and drug use found major differences between Argentina and the United States as to backgrounds and workable solutions. Her Air Force Academy's research on the inclusion of women found that, while there was discrimination at the Air Force Academy, the punishment was not as harsh as that at Annapolis or West Point. As president of Binghamton University, she increased the size of the student body and, more importantly, developed additional academic fields, including graduate programs and associated research.

Sandra Ball-Rokeach not only contributed media system dependency and communication infrastructure theory, but her style of research helped move the field to more multi-method and grounded research. Marilyn Ihinger-Tallman's family research became major contributions to family sociology classes and research throughout the country. Her time as an innovative chair of the sociology department managed to bring cohesion to her faculty, but also greatly increased the number of sociology students and majors.

As they explained their childhoods, the Troika's family backgrounds may or may not have led to their successful academic careers. All three Troika originated from nuclear families except Marilyn whose mother left when she was sixteen. Two of their families, Lois's and Sandra's, moved a lot because of their fathers' careers. Two of their fathers went to college although Marilyn's father dropped out after one year during World War I to help run the family farm. Sandra's father completed a PhD degree in physics. None of the mothers had college experience; in fact, neither Marilyn's nor Sandra's mothers finished high school. Lois's mother went to business school for her post-secondary school education. All the Troika's siblings attended college. Their family placements were different. Lois was the eldest with a much younger sister. Sandra was the second child among the four. Marilyn was the youngest of four children.

As they tell, encouragement for college ranged from Marilyn's older sister who went to Redlands University, to Lois's aunt and uncle's advice.

Sandra's mother, with a high native intelligence, spurred her to college and beyond. While the Troika gained grown stepchildren though marriage or remarriage, Marilyn was the only mother with five children. She raised them as a single parent for nine years before she remarried and gained two grown stepdaughters. Now, she now has fourteen grandchildren.

At one time, all three of these women had academic husbands in similar fields. Two of them divorced their first PhD husbands: Lois from Melvin DeFleur after seventeen years of marriage; Marilyn from Robert Ihinger after thirteen years of marriage. Lois's second husband had been an Air Force fighter pilot before their marriage in 2010. Both Sandra and Marilyn later became widows: Sandra in 1988 after twenty years of marriage to her social psychologist husband, Milton Rokeach. Marilyn became a widow in 2017 after forty-one years of marriage to Irv Tallman, also a social psychologist.

In one sense all three had were sponsored and mentored either directly or indirectly by older, more accomplished husbands. Only in a few instances did their academic work overlap that of their husbands. These women were determined to become individual specialists with their own research reputations. They each arrived in the WSU Department of Sociology in succession. Lois came to WSU with a recruited husband and then worked her way into the Department of Sociology. As a hired academic couple, unusual at that time at WSU, Lois established her own niche and independent scholarship. With her presence she subsequently facilitated and supported the hiring of Mendel Rokeach and Sandra Ball-Rokeach. Then, in turn, Lois and Sandra urged the hiring of Marilyn Ihinger-Tallman, who was initially hired without a husband. These three women, then the only women in the Department of Sociology in by the late 1970s and into the 1980s, supported and mentored each other through their professional as well as personal lives. Unlike the fears of an academic couple voting as a block on departmental matters, these strong women voted independently on proposals and other departmental issues.

By 2022, the Troika had all retired. In 1999, Marilyn took early retirement after her husband's retirement and desired resettlement in the Bay area. In 2010 Lois retired from Binghamton University before moving to the Denver area to be with her second husband. By 2021 Sandra, then a widow, retired from USC.

During their fifty-plus years as academics, these three women cracked the glass ceiling as "firsts" in so many ways. They went to college in the late 1950s and early 1960s when, in 1960, only 6 percent of female students completed undergraduate degrees. The Troika crashed through that proverbial glass ceiling and thousands of women students followed, so that now, more than half of today's undergraduate students are female.

The Troika dared to complete their doctorate degrees when two of them were the only females in their PhD programs. They had no female professors either as mentors, or members of their doctoral committees. Now, in their sociology field, female professors have reached almost parity even in the professor ranks. In 2022, out of the 1,095 US sociology professors, 49.6 percent were female. The pay gap is still there, with female sociology professors making 5 percent less pay than their male sociology colleagues, without accounting for professorial rank and years hired.[1]

All three women were a gender anomaly as full professors at Washington State University in the 1970s and 1980s. Even in 2021, an American Association of University Women (AAUW) study found that only 20.7 percent of the country's universities had tenured female full professors. It was even less at Washington State in the early 70s where only 10 percent of the full-time professors at any rank were female.

Despite being overwhelmingly filled with female undergraduates, the academic power roles remained male. Lois DeFleur's rise from dean to provost to president in less than ten years was extraordinary, especially for a woman administrator. Even in 2022 with more than 50 percent of undergraduate college students as female, the AAUW research found that this past year only 39 percent of public university deans were women. For provosts at public universities, the numbers were slightly less, with 35 percent female. And not surprisingly, female presidents of public universities were only 34 percent.[2]

The three women's stories give a set of granular collective memories of academic lives and careers as women in universities. With their varied backgrounds and family situations, they each faced many challenges and accomplished much as scholars and as leaders through shear intellect, determination, and stamina for over fifty years. They joined those few other women in their field to crash the proverbial glass ceiling as they overcame much, including sexism and nepotism rules. Their stories inspire current and beginning graduate students and professors, no matter what their field. Their accounts provide insight into the history of higher education to those curious about academic life and the changing role of women in universities.

Lois DeFleur's recounted memories point to her own personal commitment and openness for new opportunities, along with demanding work that indicate success on many fronts. She found great satisfaction with receiving grants and involving students in the research. As a professor and an administrator at all levels, Lois tells of the fulfillment she found in observing students' intellectual development and achievement. Sandra Ball-Rokeach points with pride the intellectual growth of her graduate students in the innovative Metamorphosis research project. Marilyn Ihinger-Tallman stories tell of the rewards of being organized and persistent, despite many obstacles, and receiving campus-wide rewards as a teacher while also becoming an administrator, a researcher, and mother of five highly successful children.

All three of these mighty few, this band of sisters, reflect with satisfaction of lives well-lived and now smile at the changes being made to their sub-fields, which include more than just Caucasian females, but women of color. They, Lois B. Defleur, Sandra Ball-Rokeach, and Marilyn Ihinger-Tallman, showed that the proverbial glass ceiling can be shattered even more for the entry of more diverse leaders, closer to matching the demographics of the United States and adding greatly to the field.

Notes

1. "Sociology Professor Demographics and Statistics in the US," Zippia, https://www.zippia.com/sociology-professor-jobs/demographics/. Accessed June 10, 2023.
2. *The Women's Power Gap at Elite Universities* (Harwich Port, MA: Eos Foundation, 2022), https://www.aauw.org/app/uploads/2022/01/WPG-Power-Gap-at-Elite-Universities-Full-Report.pdf.

Betty Houchin Winfield, left, with Lois B. DeFleur, Marilyn Ihinger-Tallman, and Sandra Ball-Rokeach, at a 2018 Seattle reunion.

Index

Italicized numbers indicate illustrations.

About the Authors

Betty Houchin Winfield, PhD: A child of Arkansas, my academic degrees are from the universities of Arkansas, Michigan, and Washington, followed by postdoctoral work at Columbia University and Harvard's John F. Kennedy School of Public Affairs. My professorships were at Washington State University (1979-1990) and University of Missouri (1990-2011), where I became University of Missouri Curators' Professor with appointments in the Missouri School of Journalism, the political science department, and the Harry Truman School of Public Affairs. In 2010, I was a Roy H. Park Distinguished Visiting Professor at the University of North Carolina. With over 100 academic publications, primarily in political and historical communications, I also published five books, including *FDR and the News Media* (1990, 1994). Among my awards were the student-selected WSU Faculty of the Year Award (1980), the Missouri Thomas Jefferson Award, University of Missouri Distinguished Faculty Award, the University of Washington Alumni Hall of Fame, and the Outstanding University of Arkansas Alumni Award in Education. My national/international awards include the AEJMC Cathy Covert Award for historical research, the AJHA Sidney Kobre Award for Lifetime Achievement in Journalism History, the AJHA Excellence in Teaching, and the Fulbright Distinguished Chair in American Studies at the University of Warsaw in Poland (2012). Married to academic Barry Hyman, I'm the mother of two daughters and the grandmother of five.

Lois B. DeFleur, PhD: I was born in Aurora, Illinois, but moved often while growing up. I attended a small liberal arts college in Illinois and went on to earn graduate degrees from Indiana University and the University of Illinois. After I married my sociology professor, Dr. Melvin DeFleur, we had collegiate teaching positions in Kentucky, where I became a licensed pilot and bought my first airplane. In 1967, we moved to Washington State University. With Professor William D'Antonio, we three wrote a very successful college sociology textbook, *Sociology: Human Society* through seven editions. After my marriage ended, I bought another, faster aircraft. As textbook author and pilot, I became the first female Distinguished Visiting Professor at the US Air Force Academy. Returning to WSU, I was appointed Dean of the College of Humanities and Social Sciences. In 1986, I moved to the University of Missouri at Columbia as University Provost. Four years later, I was appointed president of the State University of New York at Binghamton and served there for 20 years. I chaired the boards of the American Council on Education and the National Association of State Universities and Land-Grant Colleges and received major honors, such as the McGraw Prize in Education.

Sandra Ball-Rokeach, PhD: I was born in Ottawa, Canada in 1941. After my family immigrated to the United States, I adapted to living in many different places. Seattle became my base for graduate studies at the University of Washington. My career started at the University of Alberta and continued to change until I joined the sociology faculty at Michigan State University, where I married Milton Rokeach in 1969. We both moved to the sociology department at Washington State University in 1972, where my career took off.

My published works include seven books: *Violence and the Media; Theories of Mass Communication; The Great American Values Test; Media, Audience and Society; Paradoxes of Youth and Sport; Technological Visions;* and *Understanding Ethnic Media.*

I have published more than 100 journal articles in fields ranging from sociology and communication to information science and psychology. Many of these come out of my twenty-year Metamorphosis Project, to which more than 150 wonderful graduate students contributed.

I have been a Fellow and a Board Member in several national and international organizations, but my most prized awards are for mentoring students. They include Mellon, the University of Southern California Provost's Mentoring Award, and the International Communication Association's B. Aubrey Fisher Mentoring Award.

Marilyn Ihinger-Tallman, PhD: My life began in an unemployed household in the middle of the Great Depression. Post-war norms in America in the 1950s were my teenage models: marry, have children (I had five), be a wife and mother. I married at the age of 18. That life of thirteen years ended in 1966, when I found myself at the edge of the American upward slope of divorcing couples. As a single parent, I knew I needed to complete a college degree, which I did at the University of California, Riverside. I stayed there for my master's degree.

In 1971, I entered the doctoral program in sociology at the University of Minnesota and began work on my dissertation by 1975. Washington State University invited me to apply for an assistant professorship position and then offered the job. Within the next year, I finished and defended my dissertation and remarried. Over the next twenty-two years, I collaborated with a colleague to publish on divorce, remarriage, stepparenting, and sibling relationships. In 1987, after I was elected sociology department chair, I enjoyed promoting the department and faculty within the larger university. By 1999, I retired and co-authored with another colleague the textbook I had always wanted to write: *Families in Context* (2005).